Louise Benda
53 Nebraska Ln.
Hedgesville, WV 25427

D1065336

ONE-ROOM SCHOOL

The Western Frontier Library

ONE-ROOM SCHOOL

*Teaching in 1930s
Western Oklahoma*

by Donna M. Stephens

University of Oklahoma Press : Norman and London

Library of Congress Cataloging-in-Publication Data

Stephens, Donna M., 1940–
    One-room school : teaching in 1930s western Oklahoma /
Donna M. Stephens.
      p. cm. — (The Western frontier library ; 57)
    Includes bibliographical references and index.
    ISBN 0-8061-2313-3
    1. Morris, Helen Hussman, 1910– . 2. Women teachers—
Oklahoma—Major County—Biography.   3. Rural
schools—Oklahoma—Major County—History—Case
studies.   4. Education, Rural—Oklahoma—History—Case
studies. I. Title. II. Series.
LA2317.M578S74   1990
340.19′346′0976629—dc20   90-50240

The paper in this book meets the guidelines for permanence and
durability of the Committee on Production Guidelines for Book
Longevity of the Council on Library Resources, Inc. ∞

One-Room School: Teaching in 1930s Western Oklahoma is
Volume 57 in The Western Frontier Library.

This book is dedicated to my mother, Helen Hussman
Morris, who lived this story, and to my father,
C. A. Morris, who loved her.

CONTENTS

ILLUSTRATIONS

MAP

PREFACE

The story in this book evolved from what began as an effort to record, for my nephews and other family members, a period in the life of my parents, C. A. and Helen Hussman Morris. With the sudden and unexpected death of my father in 1985, I realized that it was important for me to write down some of the stories I had heard from my parents or these would be lost forever. While growing up in Oklahoma in the 1940s and 1950s, my brothers and I were told many times about the hardships of the Great Depression of the 1930s and about many of the difficulties our parents had encountered during their early years of marriage. One of our favorite stories involved their living in a tent across the road from the school where they were teaching because there was no other place for them to live. My father, who was a very good storyteller, took great delight in marking off a nine-by-twelve-foot area and describing the inside of the tent in detail so that we were able to imagine the small space in which they lived during that school year.

During the summer of 1986, I decided to use once again some of the research methods I had used to write my doctoral dissertation, employing them with my mother and others to capture the story about the year my parents lived in the tent. During the first two days of data collection, however, I heard about many new aspects of my mother's early life and began to realize that there was a very important and broader-based story to tell. I learned that the year in the tent had been only one of the interesting experiences my mother had had as a rural teacher. My focus changed to include as much as possible about her becoming a teacher and her experiences as one in Major County, Oklahoma, between 1929 and 1935.

In addition to the details about my mother's teaching experiences, a picture of what it was like to live in western Oklahoma in the early part of the twentieth century emerged. From tape recordings of my parents in sessions several years earlier as we looked through family photographs, from interviews with my mother and some of her former pupils, from reviews of county records and bits of writing, and from my own recollections, there evolved the story of a farm girl who, with minimal preparation, became a teacher and married her college sweetheart.

Although this is my mother's story, it is not unlike those of many other young women in that day. In 1917–18, there were 196,037 country or one-room schools in the United States. As recently as 1958–59, there were 23,695 one-room schools in this country; according to figures from the U.S. Department of Education, there were still 798 one-teacher schools in 1982–83. This book captures the memories of only one, who taught in one-room western Oklahoma schools in the early 1930s. Surely there are equally fascinating and important stories to tell about each of the communities that had one-room schools, and I consider them valuable segments of American history that need to be recorded as part of our rich heritage. As one-room school teachers and their pupils age, I believe it is important to ensure that their priceless recollections are not lost. Therefore, a major purpose of this book is to share the story of one such teacher, Helen, and thereby encourage others to record their stories of small communities served by one-room schools. This will ensure that our children's children can enjoy discovering and learning from the everyday lives of their forebears.

My own twenty-three-year career as a public-school teacher and administrator greatly influenced my interpretation of the material I collected. I noticed many similarities in my mother's concerns and frustrations about her teaching experiences from fifty years before and those of teachers with whom I worked at the time of my study. Furthermore, many of the school improvement efforts made by the Oklahoma Department of Education during the 1930s addressed concerns that were very similar to those faced by state education departments in the late 1980s. Thus my mother's story reflects her perceptions of some of the major improvement efforts during her tenure.

As I completed my study of Helen, the one-room school teacher, I was struck repeatedly by the recurring similarities of then and now, and I began to realize that her story contained valuable insights and useful information for those of us in the teaching profession and for the makers of local, state, and national education policies. As we wrestle with difficult decisions that will shape the future of public education, it is important that we understand and learn from experiences of the past.

According to futurist David Pearce Snyder, who spoke to rural educators in October 1987, futurists must base their views of the future upon a thorough understanding of history if they are going to be effective. Another purpose of this book, then, is to call attention to some of the educational issues which were present in the 1930s and which are still being addressed at the local, state, and national levels. The most important of these are recruitment and retention of good teachers, certification of teachers and the use of qualifying examinations, induction needs of teachers, appropriate preservice and in-service training, supervision and evaluation of teachers, salary and tenure for teachers, quality of teachers' work life (for example, the problem of isolation), living conditions available to teachers, community involvement in schools, the all-important student achievement tests, state-sponsored school improvement efforts, and the dilemma of policy implementation.

I challenge members of today's education and policy communities to build upon the lessons of the past, if there are to be true improvements in public education for the future. I believe that there is much to be learned from our one-room-school heritage and that there are valuable lessons to be found in Helen's experiences as a one-room-school teacher in 1930s western Oklahoma.

DONNA M. STEPHENS

ACKNOWLEDGMENTS

This book would not have been possible without the assistance of many individuals. The following people at the Major County Courthouse in Fairview, Oklahoma, were very cooperative in helping me review school records and locate old school buildings: Melvin Cornealson, court clerk; Betty Sawyer, deputy court clerk and secretary in the county superintendent's office; and Guyla Barger, secretary to the county commissioners. Former students at Orion School who were willing to share their memories with me in interviews were Leota Hedrick Louthan of Chester, Oklahoma; Alzada Gould Sharp of Seiling, Oklahoma; and Alvaretta Estes Venable of Lahoma, Oklahoma. Mr. and Mrs. Edward Kennedy of Ringwood, Oklahoma, were gracious and cooperative in sharing information about Cimarron Valley School and in welcoming us into the converted school building which is now their home. Sandy Garrett, director of rural education, and Rose C. Steve, administrator, records management, in the Oklahoma Department of Education, offered much assistance in this study by allowing me to borrow volumes from the department's archives.

I offer thanks to my family and friends who assisted and encouraged me throughout this lengthy process. Special thanks go to my friends Robert Wilson and Sue Dorcey of the University of Maryland for their help in the editing process. Especially to my husband, E. Robert Stephens, who provided encouragement, stimulation, and technical expertise, I extend my deepest appreciation.

The major sources of information for this book were my parents, C. A. and Helen Morris. Their notes, photograph albums, bits of tape recordings, and stories told to me during my childhood formed the basis of this study. My mother's assistance was invaluable as she made hours of tape recordings and accompanied me to the field sites, which generated bittersweet emotions for her. She also helped me complete the project by checking the resulting document for accuracy.

The preparation of this publication was a challenging and enjoyable effort for me, professionally and personally. I not only learned a great deal about my own family, but I also discovered a lot about myself. I strongly encourage others to capture the memories of their own families and communities.

ONE-ROOM SCHOOL

INTRODUCTION

A Brief History of Public Education in Oklahoma

THE SETTLEMENT OF OKLAHOMA

Before the United States and France negotiated the Louisiana Purchase in 1803, the 69,919-square-mile area which now makes up the state of Oklahoma was inhabited by nomadic and settled tribes of Indians. The nomads, or Plains Indians, roamed the tall, lush grass of the prairies, hunting the abundant buffalo and other game. The settled Indians tilled the soil in rich river bottoms. With the completion of the Louisiana Purchase, American explorers began mapping these lands.

After the War of 1812, the lands were seen as a potential solution to settler's problems with Indian uprisings in recently acquired areas of Florida. Oklahoma first began to receive large numbers of Indian immigrants in 1819 when the U.S. government began forcing Indians to give up their homes in the southeastern United States. The major movement of the Five Civilized Tribes (Cherokees, Choctaws, Chickasaws, Creeks, and Seminoles), which the Cherokees called the Trail of Tears, occurred from 1830 to 1843. The five tribes and a substantial number of mixed-blood established permanent homes in the eastern portion of Oklahoma, where the low mountains and wooded hills were more like their former homes than the dry plains of the west.

The relocated Indians were allotted areas for settlement and given land. They established governments of their own and became nations, with capitals and elected officials. They were helped to build schools and churches by missionaries and, to a lesser degree, by the federal government.

Many Indians in southeastern Oklahoma were slaveholders. During the Civil War, there were divided loyalties, although most Indians were sympathetic to the Confederate cause. There was bloody fighting as white Americans used the excuse of squelching the Indians' support of the Confederacy to break treaties and move the Indians off their lands. To protect Indian land, the government established military posts, which became centers for negotiating with the Plains Indians who lived in central, northern, and western Oklahoma but roamed from Texas to the Dakotas. The invention of the repeating rifle resulted in the near extinction of buffalo by white hunters, so the government began to settle the Plains tribes on reservations after 1867. These Indians' way of life was changed significantly, as they were no longer mobile and had to become dependent upon the whites for subsistence.

The coming of the railroad and the establishment of terminals in Kansas had a major effect on Indian life. Texans began to drive cattle north to the terminals, negotiating grazing leases with the Indians. During the 1870s, between four hundred thousand and six hundred thousand head of cattle were driven across the Indian land. The Missouri, Kansas and Texas Railroad reached Oklahoma in 1870, and coal was discovered in eastern Oklahoma at about the same time, which brought an increasing number of white people to the lands of the Indians.

The U.S. government obtained 1,880,000 acres in central Oklahoma from the Creek and Seminole tribes. This area, called Unassigned Lands, was surveyed and divided into townships, each containing 36 sections, or 36 square miles. By 1889 all of present-day Oklahoma, with the exception of Unassigned Lands and No Man's Land in the Panhandle, was occupied by or assigned to various Indian tribes. A number of former slaves owned land as the result of Reconstruction agreements, and this gave them full tribal citizenship and land allotments.

The Unassigned Lands were very attractive to white settlers looking for a place to homestead, and so, after much pressure, Congress passed legislation authorizing their opening. On April 22, 1889, more than fifty thousand home-seekers and adventurers, known as Boomers, lined the borders of the Unassigned Lands. At noon, a gun was fired, and horses, carriages, wagons, and people on foot poured across the line, but some folks had sneaked in before the run; these were the Sooners. By nightfall, hundreds of settlers mingled in a handful of boisterous tent cities that dotted the prairie, and thousands of farm families camped on new homesteads of 160 acres (a quarter of a section) each. Six counties were born: Oklahoma, Logan, Cleveland, Canadian, Kingfisher, and Payne.

These newly settled lands, plus Beaver County (which included all of No Man's Land in the Panhandle), were designated Oklahoma Territory by Congress in the Organic Act of May 2, 1890. The name was derived from the Choctaw words *okla,* meaning "people," and *homma* or *humma,* meaning "red." The Organic Act set up executive and judicial branches of government and provided for a delegate to Congress, a territorial legislature, and schools. Oklahoma Territory was an island of whites surrounded by Indian Territory. As new areas were opened for settlement, they were made part of Oklahoma Territory.

On September 22, 1891, the second land run took place into the Shawnee Reservation. In 1893 the government established the Dawes Commission to negotiate with the Indian tribes for their surplus land. The commission offered them allotments and then negotiated agreements for purchasing large tracts around them. Three other runs followed from 1893 to 1895, opening an additional 9,868,976 acres for settlement. These were into the Cheyenne-Arapaho Reservation, the Cherokee Outlet, and the Kickapoo Reservation. On August 16, 1901, the Kiowa-Comanche lands were opened by lottery, and in 1906 sealed bids opened an area known as the Big Pasture. By this time, Oklahoma Territory had grown substantially, diminishing the lands that had been Indian Territory.

In 1906, President Theodore Roosevelt signed the Enabling Act, combining Indian Territory and Oklahoma Territory into a single state of seventy-seven counties. Provisions of the act set aside sections 16 and 36 of each township in Oklahoma Territory for the benefit of common schools and appropriated $5 million for schools in Indian Territory. A convention adopted a constitution in July 1907, and the people ratified it two months later. On November 16, 1907, Oklahoma became the forty-sixth state.

ESTABLISHMENT OF PUBLIC SCHOOLS

When the territorial legislature held its first session in 1890, what is now the state of Oklahoma was still divided into Indian Territory and Oklahoma Territory. Although the legislature adopted the school laws of Kansas with a few modifications, the responsibility for educating children fell mainly on each community. The legislature provided for an appointed territorial superintendent of public instruction and for county superintendents. The settlers made every effort to organize one-room, one-teacher, eight-grade schools within walking distance of every rural family. Since most home-steaders were young parents with growing families, some schools overflowed with fifty or more pupils, while others had barely enough children to merit a teacher. The 1890 legislature established a normal school to prepare teachers for the rural schools and made each county superintendent responsible for certifying teachers on the basis of examinations prepared by the territorial education department.

Under the Curtis Act of 1898, the federal government assumed control of the schools in Indian Territory and appointed a superintendent. The tribes were reluctant to surrender control of their institutions, but because the secretary of the interior controlled their funds, they had little choice but to cooperate.

When Oklahoma Territory and Indian Territory were combined into the state of Oklahoma, the new constitution provided free public schools for all children in the state. It also directed that each county was to elect a superintendent, who would have authority to establish and largely control some aspects of local schools.

To keep the schoolhouse within walking distance for every child, regional districts were based on the township. Each township was divided into four parts, allowing nine square miles to a school district. In the first year of statehood (1907–1908), Oklahoma "had a total of 5,656 [school districts,] slightly over 3,400 in Oklahoma Territory and a few over 2,000 in Indian Territory."[1] Its 257,000 pupils were instructed by 6,300 teachers; before statehood, only 55 percent of the children were ever enrolled in school. The school year lasted only three to seven months.[2]

There was no serious effort to provide more than an eight-grade education because few boys and girls were serious about going to school beyond the eighth grade. In 1908 one county with nearly five thousand children in seventy-four schools graduated only forty-two of them from the eighth grade.[3] Many of the teachers were only eighth-grade graduates themselves; practically all of them had less than two years of high school work. More teachers held the county third-grade certificate, reflecting the minimum requirements on the certification tests, than any other certificate.[4]

At this time, most of the schoolhouses were one-room frame buildings lighted by windows on both sides. They were heated by a stove in the middle of the room, around which children shivered in the morning and from which they moved as far as possible in the afternoon.[5] At first, local rather than state officials were responsible for renovating old buildings, constructing new facilities, and finding competent teachers. The financial burden proved to be more than the local units could handle in the former Indian Territory, so Congress made a special appropriation of $300,000 for rural schools, which continued until 1913.[6]

State school officers were empowered to do little more than collect and disseminate information on school conditions and submit annual reports to the legislature with recommendations for improvements. It was hoped that local officials who saw their schools cast in relatively unfavorable light in the state reports would be motivated to improve them.[7]

By 1914 the number of school districts in Oklahoma had increased from 5,656 to 5,880. The 1919 legislature attempted to reduce the number of schools by giving the superintendents arbitrary power to annex school districts, allowing them to dissolve a district with fewer than eight children by annexing it to an adjoining district. County superintendents, who were elected officials, were reluctant to close schools that the communities wanted to keep, so reducing the number of school districts happened very slowly.[8]

The county superintendent was nominated by a political party every two years at the same time other county officials were elected. Training and experience as a supervisor of teachers was not a requirement for the superintendency, although state law required each county superintendent to observe procedures in each school in the county once a year. Until 1929, when statewide teacher-certifying examinations were established, county superintendents were responsible for devising as well as giving the examinations for their own teachers. There were three teaching-certificate levels based upon performance on the teachers' examination: first grade, which required an average of 90 percent with no mark below 75 percent; second grade, which required an average of 80 percent and no mark below 65 percent, with fewer academic areas required; and third grade, which required an average of 75 percent and no mark below 60 percent in even fewer academic areas. First- and second-grade certificates were valid for two years, but the third-grade certificate was good for only one year. Five-year and lifetime certificates were issued and required the completion of college credits.[9]

The county superintendents spent an ever-increasing amount of time with administrative duties. In addition to giving the examinations for certifying teachers and eighth-grade graduation, completing reports for the state superintendent, and administering state and federal aid to schools, the county superintendent also worked closely with elected local school boards. The county superintendent also had the responsibility of dividing the county into the necessary number of school districts and of using established boundary-modification procedures to conform to population changes.

THE MOVEMENT TO CONSOLIDATION

In 1908, President Roosevelt established the National Commission on Country Life to find solutions for rural problems, not the least of which was the rural school problem. The Country Life movement, whose slogan was "Better farming, better business, better living," introduced new farming and soil-conservation techniques and demonstrated the more efficient use of mechanized agricultural equipment. Its advocates, often at odds with country residents themselves, believed that country schools should be consolidated. Paved roads and the use of automobiles and school buses eliminated the need to have country schools within walking distance of every farm family with children. The Country Lifers stressed that a half-dozen one-room ungraded schools could be consolidated into one larger school with separate grades in separate classrooms. In the interest of efficiency, the movement advocated compartmentalization of education.[10]

The 1909 convention of the Oklahoma Teachers' Association in Oklahoma City urged the creation of rural high schools throughout the state. The state board of education, organized in 1911, strongly favored consolidation of rural school districts and published a bulletin, titled *Rural School Consolidation,* which outlined the procedures for consolidation and included a summary of the state's progress up to that time.[11]

The state superintendent, R. H. Wilson, asserted that farm boys and girls should have the same or equivalent advantages of education as boys and girls who lived in towns. He believed this could be brought about by grading country schools more effectively, raising teacher requirements, and providing additional instruction above the eighth grade. Superintendent Wilson believed that forming larger districts from smaller ones would equalize educational benefits. To encourage school districts to consolidate, the State Aid Act of 1911 permitted the state superintendent and state board to use the union-graded consolidated district fund to assist with school-building construction in consolidated districts.[12]

In 1913 the legislature tried to help new districts and give impetus to consolidation by appropriating $100,000 for buildings. It required that new school buildings be located centrally, that consolidated districts have an area of twenty-five square miles, and that transportation be provided for students living two or more miles from school. The legislature failed to appropriate funds for this purpose in 1915, but later sessions continued to help with construction, which promoted consolidation.[13]

TRANSPORTATION

By the time Oklahoma became a state, it had gradually begun to solve its transportation problems with a fair system of dirt roads stretching across the countryside and bridges spanning most of the larger streams. The state had constructed some permanent highways by 1915. In 1918, 86 consolidated school districts provided transportation for pupils, and by 1920 the number of districts increased to 184. Motorized vehicles gradually replaced horse-drawn wagons and in 1919 were legalized for pupil transport. Local districts did not have to provide transportation for its pupils until the General Equalization Act of 1935 made transportation part of the minimum program for Oklahoma schools.[14]

In 1920 the cost of transportation still seemed to be the major obstacle to creating large central schools. Ninety-eight consolidated districts reported that they had spent nearly 20 percent of their operating costs for this purpose.

This delayed consolidation, particularly in areas where property evaluations were extremely low and it was impossible for local school boards to meet the additional expense.[15]

During this time, the population of Oklahoma began to shift and the state was no longer strictly rural. New farming methods, better roads, and industrialization caused thousands to leave farm communities and move to industrial areas. In effect, the process of urbanization gradually pulled people away from some localities, so schools could no longer be supported and were no longer needed. In many places the school buildings remained and were used as community centers or homes.[16] The record number of 5,880 school districts in Oklahoma in 1914 was reduced to 4,450 by January 1947 and to 856 by May 1968 as the state became urbanized.[17]

FACILITIES

When Oklahoma became a state, 257,000 children were being taught in 5,600 schoolhouses worth $5.25 million. The first laws governing minimum new-school-building requirements were passed in 1919. The loss of thirty-five lives in a fire at Babbs Switch School near Hobart at Christmastime in 1924 attracted so much attention that additional safety measures were provided by statute, but no appropriations were made to enforce any of them.[18]

State Superintendent M. A. Nash, elected in 1922, worked hard to standardize rural schools throughout the state by using the Model School Score Card. About five hundred qualified as model schools in 1924, fifteen hundred districts the following year, and two thousand in 1925.[19] The score card was devised to improve the physical equipment of rural schools. Desirable playground arrangement and equipment, building standards, instructional equipment, health safeguards, school organization, and other items were on a checklist to assist school officers and teachers in assessing needed improvements.[20] Nash also recommended a minimum school term of nine months and enactment of a full-time attendance law.

INSTRUCTION

The Oklahoma Constitution of 1907 provided for what was then considered the most progressive way of choosing a textbook: the one-book, exclusive-adoption method at the state level by a commission composed of laymen and educators. An amendment in 1946 made educators assume sole responsibility for selecting and adopting multiple textbooks.[21] During the period the single statewide list of approved textbooks was in effect, only one-fifth of them were changed in any one year. This was to ensure that parents would never have to purchase a full set of textbooks.[22]

The first state courses of study were primarily content outlines and time schedules. The outlines were topical, and the sequence followed state-adopted textbooks. Few teaching suggestions or enrichment materials were included. Because printing funds were scarce, bulletins distributed to teachers were very brief. They provided assistance and structure so that the state's relatively inexperienced teachers could cover required courses systematically.[23]

In October 1929 the first comprehensive and cooperative statewide course-of-study revision was organized. The legislature appropriated a small fund for travel and clerical expenses of the various curriculum committees, and a larger sum was provided to print courses of study for elementary and high school subjects.[24] A course of study was defined as the arrangement of materials and activities of instruction in any one subject, such as English or mathematics, to serve as a helpful guide to the teacher in the classroom. The curriculum consisted of all experiences in which the pupils engage in school under the guidance of the teacher. The courses of study were to suggest the particular facts, skills, attitudes, and habits that should be emphasized and mastered in each subject and grade. Grade-level standards of mastery and methods of checking results were suggested. Teaching procedures and aids, including lists of suitable supplemental library books and instructional supplies, were included.[25]

The Division of Rural School Supervision was established by the Department of Education in the late 1920s to promote school improvement through advisory actions. State Superintendent John Vaughn, who served from 1927 to 1935, advocated the continued widespread use of the Model School Score Card, which was intended to improve the physical plants of rural schools, and the Instructional Score Card, which was developed to improve instructional programs in rural elementary schools.[26]

TEACHER PREPARATION

In its first session in 1890 the territorial legislature established a normal school to train teachers for rural schools; by the early 1930s, Oklahoma had six state teachers' colleges.[27] In 1931, under a special grant of $1,000 from the General Education Board, the director of the Division of Teacher Training was authorized to conduct an analytical study of professional courses in education offered in the various institutions. Its purpose was to determine the extent to which various subjects overlapped or duplicated one another.[28] Section 10 of Article 2 of the Oklahoma School Act of 1931 required high school inspectors to "visit all schools of college rank to familiarize themselves with the character of work being done in each institution."[29]

In the late 1920s the state director of teacher training

promoted preteaching conferences in each training institution to help beginning teachers plan for the first week's work. This plan was not successful in many of the twenty-four institutions, and in 1931 it was modified to have the preschool conferences in each county under the supervision of the county superintendent.[30] However, state officials encouraged county superintendents to continue working with training institutions.

FINANCES

The unequal distribution of wealth made state aid for schools imperative. From 1907 to 1933, school districts participated in the distribution of a statewide 0.25-mill levy, but the legislature discontinued it during the Depression to give relief to ad valorem taxpayers. Other sources of revenue were district mortgage taxes, fines for certain offenses, gross oil and gas production taxes, auto and farm truck licenses, and federal funds, which were used to support teachers of vocational subjects. These sources did little to equalize school districts' abilities to provide adequate educational programs for all students. The legislature appropriated $100,000 to help pay yearly expenses of weak schools in 1919, and succeeding legislatures increased it fivefold within six years. Under John Vaughn's superintendency, state aid to schools increased from $1,489,762 in 1927–28 to $8,180,000 in 1935–36.[31]

The chief weakness of early efforts to equalize assistance to education was that no objective method had been developed to distribute the funds. The districts that made their desires known in the most forceful manner frequently received funds, leaving less-assertive and perhaps needier districts with little or no state aid.[32] Furthermore, the economic condition of each local school district directly affected the teacher in its school. The salaries of rural teachers were paid by the clerks of local school boards with warrants drawn on the district funds, which at times were very low. Banks always checked a school district's balance before redeeming the warrants. If funds were insufficient, the bank gave the teacher the option of holding the warrant to collect interest until such time as the district could redeem it or cashing the warrant at a 20 percent loss and letting the bank profit by the difference and interest.[33]

CONCLUSION

During the forty-five years from the birth of Oklahoma Territory in 1890 until the end of State Superintendent John Vaughn's tenure in 1935, many technological advances were made in every aspect of the lives of Oklahoma citizens. Intensive efforts were made to improve public education and equalize educational opportunities for all children in the state.

For the early settlers of Oklahoma and for those who continued to live in the rural areas through the Great Depression, life was difficult. It was not easy to maintain a local school when the district's families could hardly feed themselves. However, the education of their children was a high priority for most parents, and the local school played an important role for all citizens in the community. Each year they scraped together enough money to hire a teacher and hold classes for at least a few months.

The story which follows is about an Oklahoma farm girl who became a one-room-school teacher in western Oklahoma in the early 1930s. It will involve many of the major stages in the evolution of Oklahoma public education as she saw and lived them.

PROLOGUE

Helen was born to John and Stella Hussman on a blustery, cold New Year's Day 1910 on Indian land near Fonda, Oklahoma. The state of Oklahoma had been established only three years before with the joining of Oklahoma Territory and Indian Territory. The family had two other children: Laurena, born in 1906, and Ernie, born in 1908. They shared a small three-room wooden house with Stella's cousin and her husband and small daughter, who had come to Dewey County by wagon from Kansas to help John with the farm work.

John Hussman farmed and raised cattle on eight hundred acres of land that belonged to the Cheyenne and Arapaho Indians. Because the members of these tribes historically had been hunters, not farmers, they hired farmers to cultivate their land. John had been hired to farm through the Cheyenne-Arapaho Indian Agency, which represented members of both tribes and had headquarters at Cantonment, a small Indian post near Canton, Oklahoma. This post was active from 1879 to 1917.

With the profits that John and Stella were able to save, they bought a quarter section of raw land two miles east and one mile south of Seiling. They began to make plans for their new house soon after Helen was born, because the little house was becoming very crowded. Although Stella's cousin's little girl had died of an undisclosed illness, the cousin had given birth to another daughter in July 1910. Most of the early homes in that area of Oklahoma were made of sod or wood; however, John wanted to have a substantial home for his growing family, so he began to mold concrete blocks by hand to build the two-story, eight-room farm house he had planned. Late in 1910, the Hussman family moved into their home, which became a landmark in Dewey County. A large barn and other farm improvements were soon added.

In 1914 another daughter, Donna, was born. The six-member family lived a busy and active life in the spacious farmhouse. John had been able to stop working for the Indian agency and devote all of his efforts to his own farm. Stella's cousin and her family returned to Kansas when John stopped working for the Indians, although they did correspond and visit the Hussmans often.

The natural rhythm of the Hussmans' farm life was structured around planting and harvest and the seasons of the year. It was punctuated by the activities of the large extended family and activities of the small town and community. John, who had come to Oklahoma from Iowa, and Stella, who was the daughter of a general-store owner in Lahoma, Oklahoma, were very active in the community and had a constant stream of guests in their home. They tried to take their children to all activities which occurred in the community. Seiling, the closest town, was the trading center for farm families who had settled in that area.

As Helen was growing up, her brother, Ernie, suffered from asthma and could not help John with the farm work. Stella, who was usually energetic and active, suffered from lack of adequate medical attention related to her childbear-

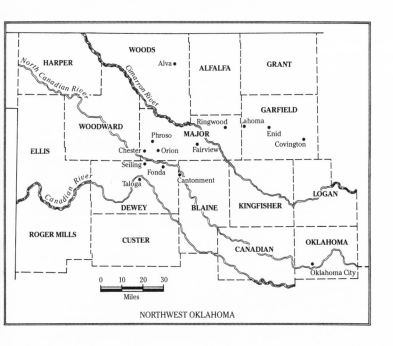

NORTHWEST OKLAHOMA

ing. Consequently, during Helen's early years her mother was not well much of the time, and the oldest daughter, Laurena, was needed to help run the large and busy farm home. The youngest child, Donna, was too small to help with the hard farm work. Thus, it fell to Helen to become her father's helper in the fields and with the heavy work that had to be done around the barn. A series of farmhands, cousins, and nephews came for short periods to help, but from Helen's earliest years she was John's long-term helper.

John used horses to cultivate 320 acres of land that was used to grow grain. He leased 160 acres that adjoined his land from his Indian neighbors. In addition, he raised sheep, cattle, hogs, geese, turkeys, and chickens. The family was self-sufficient, buying few things from the stores in nearby Seiling.

Although it was physically strenuous and exhausting, Helen enjoyed working with her father and they developed a very close and special relationship. Many times Helen and John spent twelve to fourteen hours in the field, where each of them stood behind four-horse teams which pulled the farm equipment. Plowing, planting, and harvesting took a long time using horses.

Helen was well aware of the hard work that her mother and sisters were involved in at the house. Cooking, sewing, washing, ironing, and keeping the house was not an easy job because everything had to be done by hand. Their life was not all work, however. In the evenings under carbide lights, the family played games, listened to someone play the piano, talked with visitors, and enjoyed the special sweets that Stella and Laurena prepared.

In the winter, Laurena, Helen, and Ernie, if he felt well, went with their father after supper to run his traps. John carried the lantern and the children carried gunnysacks to bring back the animals. They usually found opossums or skunks in the traps. John skinned them and sold the hides. Many people made their living by trapping at that time. If an opossum were still alive in the trap, John would kill it and Ernie would take it to sell to the schoolteacher the next day.

On winter weekends when the ground was covered with snow, the children went rabbit hunting with their dad. John would station himself at one end of a draw and the children would run down the other end, whooping and hollering. This scared the rabbits so that they would run by John, who would shoot them. That evening they would have rabbit for supper. Stella would steam the rabbit to make it tender and fix a gravy with raisins and vinegar. The sweet-and-sour rabbit and homemade bread tasted very good on those cold winter evenings.

In the summer after harvest, the Hussman family and other neighbor families would go down to the river for a three- to four-day outing. The Hussmans put a mattress in the back of their Model T truck to make a bed for Stella and the children. During the days, the children in cut-off overalls, swam and played in the North Canadian River. The women did handwork, caught up on the gossip, and cooked over the campfire. The men fished and enjoyed some free time, although they had to go back to the farms for night and morning chores.

During the summer, the North Canadian had very little running water. There were large depressions in the riverbed which formed natural swimming holes for the children and natural traps for fish. The men and boys used seines and got enough fish for everyone. Later, the use of seines was against the law, but the fish were trapped by nature in the North Canadian and usually died before the rains came. When the rains did come in late August or early September, the river became treacherous.

At other times during the summer, Helen went trotline

fishing with her dad. They would fish all night. John set the line and baited the hooks. Helen carried the bait bucket, filled with frogs they cut up for bait. After the hooks were baited, John and Helen would lie down on the cool, sandy bank to sleep. John would put his arm over Helen to make sure that his active daughter wouldn't get up while he slept. After a couple of hours, John would rouse Helen and they would run the line, taking off fish, putting them in wet gunny sacks, and rebating the hooks. They would then settle down for some more sleep. By morning they would take the fish by the house, eat breakfast, and go to work on the farm.

On one of their fishing expeditions, John told Helen they were going to try something different. Instead of a trotline and little frogs in a bait bucket, John had several jugs. He gave Helen a gunnysack and told her to jump into the water when he did and to fill her sack with fish as fast as she could.

John threw something from one of the jugs into the water and he and Helen jumped into the water. The chemicals exploded and the fish came to the surface. Helen grabbed the fish and put them in her sack as fast as she could; however, the explosives in the water stung her legs and hands like a swarm of bees. Although they got a lot of fish this way, Helen was glad when John returned to using the trotline.

Sometimes as they waited for the time to run the trotline, John noodled for fish along the bank. He would go along the bank feeling for fish with his hands. When he caught one, he handed it back to Helen to put it in a sack. However, once John reached into a muskrat's hole and the animal bit the unwelcome hand severely. There was also the ever-present danger of grabbing a snake, for water moccasins were fairly common in the North Canadian River. The Hussman family enjoyed eating the fish from those fishing expeditions. Stella and Laurena salted and canned fish so it could be enjoyed during the winter, too.

The families and individuals who lived around Seiling considered themselves part of a total community. The community dances were an important part of community social life, and John and Stella Hussman attended as often as they could. Stella, who had been raised in town, was not used to the hard work of a farm wife. Bearing and caring for four young children in rural Oklahoma was a difficult and taxing job. Although she was an excellent cook and housekeeper and loved to be around people, she suffered much from monthly body changes. John, on the other hand, had grown up on a farm in Iowa. The six-foot German seemed to thrive on hard work and excitement. At the neighborhood dances he was an often-sought-after partner. His quick wit and relatively well-traveled youth made him the center of attraction, and he loved that role. While the children were young, they usually went to sleep before the dance was over, and John would carry, them, half-asleep, to their ride back home.

During the summer of 1918, the Hussman family decided to go on a major trip with one of their neighbor families to the Cave of the Winds in Colorado. The Hussmans had a Model T Ford touring car, and their neighbors had a Buick touring car. They took tents and camped while they saw the sights of Colorado. John, Stella, and Laurena joined the other couple in walking up Pikes Peak. Helen and the other small children stayed at camp. After that grueling climb, they were ready to return to the flatlands of Oklahoma.

From winter until early spring, Helen and her brother and sisters attended the local school. When she was seven and a half, Helen started to attend the one-room school one and three-quarters miles from her home. She walked with Ernie and Laurena, who also attended. At that time, there was a six-month school term, with students from six to sixteen years old in all eight grades. Helen's early impression of the school was influenced by some of the older boys, who would smoke in the back of the room: cornsilk, tea, wild weeds, and tobacco when they could get it. The young teacher tried to control their behavior, but the older pupils did not pay her much mind.

Helen enjoyed the programs that were held at the school. She especially enjoyed the pie and box suppers that were held to raise money for the school. For the box suppers, the women and girls would prepare food and put it in a box they had decorated. The boxes were auctioned to the men and boys. Usually, the prettier the box, the higher the bid—and also the better the food. The buyer then shared the food with the woman or girl who had prepared it. Young men would try to buy the box of the lady that they wanted to spend the evening with.

Stella was known for her good food and also was very creative. For one of the box suppers, she made a box into a miniature house, with lace curtains at the windows. Young Helen watched with mixed feelings as her mother's box brought the highest price that evening. She was proud that her mother's box brought in so much money for the school, but oh, how Helen wished that she could have had that little house for her very own!

During World War I, the school was a very active place which reflected the surge in patriotism. There were many money-making projects to buy essential things and gifts for the local boys who were going to war. The school's evening programs consisted of patriotic songs, plays, and readings. When the first group of new soldiers left Seiling on their way to the nearest railroad station, Helen, her teacher, and the other students walked four miles to the main road to wave good-bye as the trucks carrying the men from the community passed.

Most of the pupils in the one-room school studied hard, but they also enjoyed the opportunity to play with the other children. At recess and at lunchtime, the children broke into groups according to age and sex. The little girls played house, laying out their house plans with sticks and pieces of wood. They brought pieces of broken dishes from home to add to their play. The young boys played marbles. The older pupils played crack-the-whip, kick-the-can, blackman, dare-base, and hide-and-seek. Annie-over was a very popular game in which groups of students got on each side of the schoolhouse. Someone from one group threw a ball over the schoolhouse, and a person from the other group was to catch it and run around the schoolhouse and touch the opposite wall without being caught. Some of the games became very rough.

Helen shared a desk with a girl named Esther Short-nose, a Cheyenne-Arapaho. Her family lived one-half mile south of Helen on a quarter section deeded to the family by the U.S. government. Esther's grandparents had been hunters, and when the Indian lands were divided, they were restricted to their farm. Since they were not farmers, Helen's dad leased their farm to cultivate and run livestock. The children played together along the creek bank that separated their properties.

Esther showed her friendship for Helen by giving Helen a pair of white beaded buckskin moccasins that her mother had made for Helen's doll. Helen's sister Donna became good friends with Esther's cousin Wisdom Nibbs, who was Donna's age. When the Nibbs family went by the Hussman farm in their wagon, Donna and Helen would wave and shout hello. However, Wisdom would duck down, embarrassed by the girls' attention.

The rural teacher was responsible for planning a monthly literary. The Hussmans had attended these meetings for years. The evening usually consisted of a short program by the children, followed by some type of program planned by the teacher and some members of the community. Debates were very popular while Helen was in school. These were judged and were a highlight of the community's activities.

In 1922, Helen and her sisters and brother began attending school at Seiling. A Model T truck with benches and a roof, and canvas sides in the winter, came by on the dirt road in front of their house and took them the seven miles to the consolidated school at Seiling. There were separate classes for the eight grades and also a high school. Although learning in school did not come easily for Helen, she was very conscientious and was a good student.

Since the Seiling schools were not accredited by the state of Oklahoma, students had to pass the county examinations at the end of their seventh- and eighth-grade years.[1] The seventh-grade examinations covered Oklahoma history, civics, home economics or agriculture, and physiology. Students had two chances to pass the eighth-grade examinations in arithmetic, reading, grammar, spelling, penmanship, history, and geography. The first opportunity to pass was in March and the last chance was in May. In March of her eighth-grade year, Helen passed all of her examinations, although she made only 65 percent in Oklahoma history. She was very disappointed in herself.

At home, Stella was quite ill and Laurena had left home to be a seamstress in a nearby town. Helen asked her teacher if she would help her study so she could retake the test and improve her score in Oklahoma history. The teacher told Helen that the only important thing was that she had passed. She informed Helen that her time had to be spent with those pupils who had not passed. Helen stayed at home, helping her mother and her father, for the remainder of that school year.

O N E

HELEN BECOMES A TEACHER

As she helped her parents on the farm, Helen began to realize that she did not want to work on the farm the rest of her life. From the time she was a small child, she had dreamed of becoming a nurse. She knew she would have to finish high school and then go to a teaching hospital to study. She had seen the hospital in Enid when she had visited her grandparents who lived near there. Because she did not have a way to make any money, she knew she would have to depend on her family to help her. Helen kept this dream as she started back to high school that fall.

During Helen's freshman year in high school, John became very ill with malaria and had to spend several months in the hospital at Enid. When he returned home, John sat Helen down and told her she could not become a nurse. He told her it was too hard a life and he did not want her to live like that. This was a blow to Helen. There weren't many jobs for young women in small towns. Her older sister, Laurena, was working as a telephone operator. There were a few jobs working in stores, but Helen was not excited about that. She continued high school with a heavy heart.

During Helen's junior year in high school, the Seiling superintendent of schools announced that he wanted any

27

students who were interested in becoming teachers to work as substitute teachers in the grade-school classes; and told them they would be paid for their work. Helen saw this as an opportunity to make some money of her own. She substituted in a few classes for teachers who were absent, and she enjoyed it. Then the first-grade teacher became very ill. The superintendent asked Helen to take over the class. For six weeks Helen was the teacher, keeping up with her own studies in the evenings. When the time came to take class pictures, the superintendent told Helen she should take her place with the first-grade class as its teacher.

It seemed to be a perfect match. Helen loved the children, she was able to keep up with her own work, and she was making some money of her own. She and her parents began to talk about what she needed to do to become a teacher.

Helen did not think of herself as a beauty, nor did she consider herself unattractive. Much of her social life had been spent with her family as they went to the dances which were held in the homes of various community members almost every Saturday night. Helen danced with the neighbor boys and often went to parties which included the young people of the community, as well as new farmhands or new young men working in town. Although she dated a number of young men, she did not have a special beau. Unlike many young women in the community who had already married or were planning to marry soon, Helen was free to make plans for her life without considering the possibility of an upcoming marriage.

For the most part, the Hussman home was a wonderful place to live and to grow up. Stella had taught all of her daughters the homemaking skills of cooking and sewing and the importance of taking good care of the family. However, the difficult farm work and long hours, and the camaraderie Helen developed with her father and the farmhands allowed her to approach life in a very special way. About once a month, the Hussmans would drive to Lahoma to see Stella's parents, who had run a mercantile store. The Hussman children were very close to their grandparents.

Helen continued to substitute-teach throughout the rest of her high school experience. Her sister Laurena had a friend, Mable Bateman, who was married and had been a teacher since leaving high school. She had taken the county examination and had been certified to teach.[1] Helen often talked to Mable about her desire to become a teacher, and Mable encouraged Helen to begin preparing for the examination.

At that time, in 1928–29, an individual who could pass the county examination could be certified with a third-, second-, or first-grade certificate and was eligible to teach for one or two years, depending on the certificate. The examinations were written and graded by the county superintendent. A bill passed by the 1929 legislature changed Oklahoma law to standardize teacher examinations throughout the state, but the law did not take effect until October 11, 1929.

In January of 1929, while still a senior at Seiling High School, Helen made the decision to take the two-day county examination. Her sponsor, Mable, was planning to take the three-day examination for her first-grade certificate and invited Helen to make the trip to the county seat at Fairview with her.

Mable had become good friends with Cleveland Weaver, the county superintendent, who was a bachelor and lived in Fairview with his mother. Mable arranged for Helen to stay over with her at the Weaver's house. Because the superintendency was an elected office, it was not un-usual for Mr. Weaver to extend hospitality to his constituents. Mable and Helen slept on the divan in the living room and ate their meals in the small café down the street from the house.

When they arrived at the county courthouse, Helen, and the other fifteen candidates paid the two-dollar fee[2] and took their places in the examination room. Their previous experiences with the seventh- and eighth-grade examinations helped them deal with their anxieties. The candidates were given no special instructions or explanation; they were just handed the questions for the first day and told to do their best.

Helen proceeded through the first categories confidently. At lunchtime they turned in their papers and tried to relax. In the afternoon session, Helen moved to the category of music. She had been exposed to music at the dances she had attended in the community. Her sister Donna was an excellent pianist, and Helen loved to listen to her play. However, the questions dealt with music theory. Helen completed the questions as best she could. With her fragile confidence shaken, she finished the first day of testing. That evening Mable assured her that no one was expected to know everything about every category. However, as she tried to go to sleep that night, Helen wondered whether she would have to give up her dream of becoming a teacher.

The next morning, she returned to the examination with renewed determination. In her work with her family on the farm, she had never been a quitter. She resolved to do her very best on the remaining examinations. She felt much better as she finished the second day of testing. The material seemed much more familiar to her, and the day went quickly. That evening Helen tried to keep from becoming overconfident. Her mother had always warned her not to count her chickens before they hatched. She would have to wait to hear the results from Mr. Weaver; in the meantime, she felt a great relief that the two-day examinations were over.

While waiting for Mable to finish her examinations on the third day, Helen sat in the superintendent's office and looked at the courses of study, the textbooks, and teaching materials that he had in his office. That evening, she and Mable returned to Seiling. Helen felt that she had learned a great deal, regardless of the outcome of the examinations. She had been told the results would be mailed to her in a couple of weeks.

Helen returned to finish high school. She tried to think of what she would do if she hadn't passed. She could continue to work on the farm with her mother and father, but she couldn't imagine a future for herself there. She waited each day for the mail. The announcement finally arrived. She had passed! She had received a third-grade teaching certificate.

The county superintendent sent a booklet to each of the candidates who passed, listing all of the schools in the county by classification. Helen quickly looked at all the third-class schools; all of them were one-room schools. The booklet also listed the salaries for each. She discovered that she could make eighty dollars per month in any of them. That evening Helen was the honored person at the Hussman dinner table. John and Stella looked over the list of possible schools with great interest. They wanted to keep their daughter as close to home as possible.

Helen continued her senior year with a flurry of activities. There were parties, picnics, and the weekly dances. However, in the back of her mind was the undefined vision of the school that she hoped to get.

In March, a letter arrived from Mr. Weaver, suggesting that Helen interview with the board of Orion School, about fourteen miles northeast of Seiling. She was very excited about this prospect because the school was close enough that she could easily come home to the farm on weekends. John and Stella were also pleased and encouraged Helen to respond quickly and tell the superintendent she would like to meet with the school board.

On the morning the interview had been arranged, Helen dressed with care. She put on the dress her mother had just made for her, carefully waved her hair, and brushed her shoes to a shine. John had agreed to take her to the interviews. They had a list of the three school-board members and directions to their homes. The interviews were to be held separately at the home of each board member.

John encouraged his daughter as they drove to the first house. He told Helen that she could do the job and that she should just go in there and tell them she could. With shaky knees, Helen went into the first house and answered the questions the best she could. When she returned to the Model T, she had gained in confidence. The questions had not been difficult, and she felt that she had done very well. She told her dad that Mr. Hedrick had not asked her any questions about music theory. They laughed as they drove to the next house.

Helen went into the next interview without fear. She returned to her father in a short while and directed him to the last school-board member's house. During the last interview, Mrs. Cossell asked Helen about her plans for living arrangements if she got the job. Helen responded that she had not thought that far ahead. Mrs. Cossell suggested that Helen could board with her for twenty dollars a month—if she got the job.

Helen was filled with enthusiasm as she and her father made the seventeen-mile trip back to the farm. She felt that each of the interviews had gone well and that Orion School would be a perfect place for her to work. She even had a place to stay.

In a few days Helen received a letter stating that she had been hired by the Orion school board. She had not yet completed her senior year of high school and she already had a job. She was very proud of herself. She realized that she would be in a position to pay her own way beginning in September.

The summer of 1929 was filled with activity and excitement. The work had to be done on the farm, but Helen's mind was on the new career that had opened up to her. She contacted Mable, who was pleased but not surprised that Helen had been hired that fall. Helen began to think about teaching in a one-room school with children in all eight grades. She talked to Mable every chance she got. One of the first things Helen had to buy was a teacher's bell. Because the one-room schools were deserted from May until September, they were a target for vandals. The handbells would be taken if they were left at the school, so each teacher was expected to bring a bell.

As Helen helped with the harvest, Laurena, who was now an experienced seamstress, made her several new dresses for her new teaching career. Helen did have to make one trip to meet with her school board to sign the contract and to take the oath required of all teachers in Oklahoma.[3] On that trip she thought to go by to see her new school.

Orion School was situated on a sandhill on the south side of a very sandy road. No one lived near the school. A deep canyon and many blackjack oak trees were on the north side of the road. The land in the area around the school was not good for farming or for ranching. The people who lived in the district were relatively poor.

As Helen got out of the car and waded through the

sandburs growing in the schoolyard, she could hardly wait to peek through the windows. Actually, Orion was quite primitive when compared to other schools in the state. Few changes had occurred at Orion since it was established on May 14, 1895.[4] Helen was reminded of the one-room school she had attended before Seiling had consolidated and the building had been moved away. Orion was a one-room clapboard structure with a high-pitched roof. The major sources of light were the windows on both sides of the room; thin, once-white curtains covered the bottom panes. A wood-burning stove stood in the middle of the room, its long stovepipe reaching the chimney behind the teacher's desk. By squinting through the window, Helen could see an ancient chalkboard on the wall behind the teacher's desk, flanked by faded pictures of George Washington and Abraham Lincoln. The desk for the teacher was on a platform raised above the floor about three inches.

Helen tried to imagine how it would be when the room was filled with children. She hoped the school board would clean the building as it had said they would do. She walked around the school and noted that the water ran from the roof in a pipe to the cistern during the rainy season. This was the only source of drinking water for the school. A woodpile and two old outhouses were the only man-made signs in the sandy schoolyard.

Helen returned home filled with ideas for sprucing up the schoolroom. She had learned that the community had been named for the mythical Greek hunter who was placed among the stars and had become an easily recognizable constellation. How romantic, she thought, to teach in a school named for a Greek character. However, the Oklahoma speech pattern altered the pronunciation to OR-ion. None of that seemed to matter to Helen; nothing could dampen her enthusiasm.

Her father had been doing some checking on the community. He learned there were many stories about the school area. One story accepted as true had to do with the activities of rustlers who lived in the canyon north of Orion. There was a cave the rustlers had dug high above one of the intersections in the canyon. The rustlers would bring stolen cattle into the canyon and secure them in a boxed-off area. They would then wait in the cave, watching for anyone who might be following them. The cave was straight for a few feet and then cut back sharply, making it impossible for anyone to shoot the rustlers, who could hide around the bend in the cave.

The leader of the band of rustlers had been run out of the area several years before, but the young men in the community made sport of exploring the cave. There were stories of gold that had been left and the rustlers who would come back to get it. Since this was diamondback-rattler territory, the concern about snakes added to the daring and excitement of exploring the cave. The lure of danger and stashed gold was enough to get many young men to take the dare and crawl up into the cave.

It was into this canyon that John brought his nineteen-year-old daughter Helen in September 1929 as she began her first job as the teacher of the school on the rim of the canyon. As they turned off the main road to go down the steep driveway to Mrs. Cossell's house that Sunday afternoon, Helen realized that she had not really paid much attention to the house in which she would be living when she had come for the interview the previous spring. It seemed so long ago.

John and Helen pulled up in front of the small log house among the scrub-oak trees at the side of the canyon bottom. There was a little open space where some livestock could be seen. John reminded Helen that he would be there to pick her up on Friday right after school. Helen took her suitcase from the Model T, kissed her father good-bye, and with butterflies in her stomach but excitement in her heart knocked on the door. This was certainly different from the large two-story stone farm home on the open plains where she had grown up.

Helen could hear voices coming from within the house, and then Mrs. Cossell opened the door. Helen had liked her looks the first time she saw her. Although Mrs. Cossell was as tall as Helen and was stockily built, not small and frail like Helen's mother, she radiated a motherly warmth. She wore her gray hair pulled back in a bun in the style most older women favored and wore an apron over her dress. Helen could see that the one big room was filled with young men. Mrs. Cossell had three sons who were in their teens and early twenties, and they had several of their friends at the house that afternoon.

Helen knew that young single female schoolteachers were much sought after. If the teacher was halfway decent-looking, she was considered a real prize by single men. Helen knew the young men were there to look her over. As she set her suitcase in the corner, she could hear her father's Model T making the steep grade out of the canyon and onto the road. She took a deep breath and began to look around. The house was basically one room in which there were two small beds, one in one corner and one in another. There was a ladder fastened to the wall above one of the beds. Later Helen would discover that the ladder leading to the loft where the three boys slept was over her bed. There was a table and some chairs near the opening which led to the lean-to kitchen. The wood cookstove furnished the heat, and there were kerosene lamps for lights. There was an outhouse in the trees behind the house.

The young men stayed and stayed. Helen thought they

would never leave so that she could go to bed. Her experiences working with the farmhands, being around her cousins and older brother, and spending many hours talking with her father allowed Helen to be at ease in a rather difficult situation. Finally, the friends left and the three Cossell boys crawled up the ladder to their beds in the loft. Helen was so tired that she went to sleep immediately when she got into bed.

Helen was awakened the next morning by the sound of Mrs. Cossell putting wood into the stove to make breakfast. This would be her first day at her very own school. Helen dressed quickly, poured some water into the washpan to wash her face, and quickly ran a comb through her bobbed hair. She ate breakfast as soon as it was ready and without paying too much attention to the three sets of eyes on her, grabbed her lunch, and started up the driveway to the road which led to the school. Before she left the house, Mrs. Cossell gave her the skeleton key that would unlock the school door.

Helen would soon be told about a shortcut through the floor of the canyon which had been made by children going to school. However, on that first day she walked the two miles along the road. Once she left the canyon and began to walk along the sandy road, the terrain that lay ahead of her looked much different from the area along the canyon. There were scrub blackjack oak trees along the ravines and in clumps on the rolling, sandy hills. Some tall grasses which were whitish-brown from the scorching dry summer waved in the breeze. The landscape was dotted with sagebrush still anchored by shallow roots in the sandy soil. Much of it had broken loose from its mooring in the severe late-summer winds and rolled "clean to Kansas" as her father liked to say.

Helen's walk was one and one-half miles south, roughly

parallel to the canyon, and one-half mile west. The canyon ended shortly before it got to the road. The road continued on to Chester, although it was passable only in good weather and when the sand didn't get too deep.

As she walked in the early morning silence, Helen could hear only the cooing of doves that were in trees along the canyon's edge and the poof, poof, poof of her footsteps in the fine sand of the roadbed. She remembered the teachers meeting held the week before at the county superintendent's office. She had gone to the meeting not knowing exactly what would be expected of her. She knew that her new school would be very different from her substitute-teaching experience in Seiling. She had tried hard to remember what the teacher had done when she attended the one-room school near her home.

At the meeting, Mr. Weaver gave the teachers what was referred to as a peptalk. He told them that Oklahoma's schools were improving rapidly and that they were going to be a part of an exciting change. In that year, he said, 2,600 of the 4,933 school districts in the state had one-teacher schools. Mr. Weaver gave the new teachers a copy of the course of study for elementary grades. It was basically an outline of what should be taught at each grade, and it had time line for preparing the seventh- and eighth-grade pupils for county examinations in the spring. Helen knew that a teacher was judged by the number of her students who passed the county examinations. If any pupils failed, the teacher would not be rehired the next year.

At first the task seemed overwhelming—all eight grades and the county examinations in the spring. Helen remembered looking at her mentor, Mable, and showing her concern in her eyes. Mable had smiled and nodded that she knew how Helen felt, but it could be done. Mr. Weaver continued by explaining that one method of covering the required material was to have the pupils make notebooks outlining all of the material from the state-required textbooks, which were the bases for the county examinations.[5] He had listed the subjects to be taught: agriculture, orthography, reading, penmanship, English grammar, physiology and hygiene, geography, U.S. history and civics, and arithmetic.[6] There were a number of other subjects which were to be woven in with the others, for example, the evil effect of alcohol; morals; human kindness; and reverence for the flag.[7]

The superintendent had emphasized the importance of observing the compulsory-attendance laws and maintaining good records.[8] Mr. Weaver had proudly announced that during the previous year, 1928–29, 11,255 rural children were neither absent nor tardy.[9]

Finally, he had reminded the teachers about the need to watch diligently for safety hazards in their schools. He reminded them of the horrible Babbs Switch fire of Christmas 1924, in which thirty-five people died because the doors opened inward and they could not escape when a fire started inside during an evening program. The teachers were cautioned to make sure there was no kerosene near the stove and not to have candles of any type in the schoolhouse.[10]

In the packet Mr. Weaver gave to each teacher were registers and records.[11] There were also lists of the holidays and special days to be observed: Temperance Day, the Friday nearest January 16; Arbor Day, the Friday following the second Monday in March; and the regular holidays.[12]

Mr. Weaver had told them he would be out to visit each of their schools during the next term.[13] As Helen left the meeting, she had felt overwhelmed. However, Mable soon alleviated some of her concerns by volunteering to help her work on her notebooks and to give her ideas to keep the children busy as she listened to the recitations of the others.

Helen had made good use of the time remaining before school started.

On her way to school on that September morning in 1929, Helen carried a bag containing the packet of materials from the superintendent, some of the materials she had begun to develop, and her teacher's bell. She hoped the books from the previous teacher and the materials purchased by the school board would be in the schoolroom.[14]

When Helen walked up the driveway toward the school, it was not yet 8:30. Although school did not start until nine o'clock, some of the children had already begun to arrive. Most of the pupils walked a mile or more to school, and many of them were barefoot; they saved their shoes for the cold weather in winter. The ground was covered with sandburs, but their toughened feet allowed the children to scrape off the stickers like mud off a boot. The children carried their books, many of them handed down from older brothers or sisters, and their lunch buckets. They had been anxious to see the new schoolteacher, and most were happy to have relief from the difficult labor they had been involved in at home. Helen unlocked the door and pulled it open. She saw the stacks of new materials on the teacher's desk and could tell that the room had been cleaned recently. By nine o'clock, she had sixteen pupils with all eight grades represented in her schoolroom.

In the back of the room was the shell of an old organ which had been gutted many years before. The children's lunch pails were kept inside the cavity. There were hooks on a board fastened to the wall for the children's coats in the winter. In the corner in the back of the room was a table with a bucket and a dipper for the drinking water.[15] One of the girls offered to get a pail of water from the pump in the cistern. Helen hoped that enough water was left in the cistern after the dry summer to get them by until the rains came in late September. She was relieved to find that the school had been cleaned, although it still looked a little dreary.

As the children had filed into the room, they took their seats according to size: the older, larger pupils sat in the back double desks and the smaller beginners sat in the front smaller desks. There was much chatter among the pupils. Although they lived within three miles of one another, they had not been together over the summer. Helen busied herself getting her desk and the rest of the room arranged to her liking.

All of a sudden she was aware of silence in the room. She looked up and saw sixteen pairs of eyes on her and began to realize the great responsibility that she had assumed. Aside from some help she hoped to get from Mable on weekends, she was basically on her own.[16] Helen knew she must divide the pupils according to grades and classes based on their previous work, decide on the order in which the classes would be taught and a schedule for recitation and study, establish routines, and inform the pupils of her rules for the school. But first she wanted to get to know her pupils. After all, she had been out of school only three months and her much-beloved little sister was about the same age as the older girls in the school.

Helen had each student stand and tell his or her name and what grade he or she was in. There was much giggling and squirming as the children introduced themselves to their new teacher. Some of the older boys in the back of the room mumbled their names and grades and quickly sat down. One boy did not stand at all. The children called their new teacher Miss Helen, which showed respect and also helped differentiate her name from that of one of the older girls who was also named Helen. The rest of the morning was spent getting settled and finding out who had the correct books and who would need to borrow or buy books for that year's work. Because the state textbook-adoption plan brought in new books on a rotating basis, most children used books from an older brother or sister unless a new book in the subject was required. As Helen looked at the children she realized that their parents probably had very little money to buy them books or clothes, and none of the families had the kinds of things that she and her brother and sisters had come to expect as necessary. She realized that she would have to work hard not to make judgments about the children and their families.

Helen organized her reading classes first. She explained that she would call the beginners first to the recitation bench, which was in the front of the room and faced the teacher's desk. While each recitation group worked with the teacher, the other pupils would read in their books or copy from the blackboard into their notebooks. For this first day Helen just had them walk through the procedures of recitation, memorizing, copying, and reading.[17] Because there were students in all eight grades, the procedures were very complex.[18]

About midmorning, the older boy in the back of the room who had not stood when he introduced himself announced that it was time for recess. All of the children looked at Miss Helen, waiting to see how she would handle Louis. The man who had been the previous teacher had not gotten along with Louis at all. On more than one occasion, the two of them had become involved in physical struggles as the teacher tried to make Louis do what he said. Miss Helen looked at the class and then looked at Louis and smiled. She said, "I do believe that it is time for recess. Go on outside and enjoy yourselves."[19]

The boys scrambled madly for the door and tumbled out onto the sandy schoolyard that was covered with stickers. The little girls ran out as soon as the dust had settled a little. However, the older girls remained inside the school. They wanted to find out more about their new teacher. Quickly they began to talk about a variety of things. For Helen it was not much different from the conversations she had with her sister Donna.

Soon it was time to ring the bell for the end of recess. As Miss Helen stood at the schoolhouse door ringing it, she really felt like a teacher.

Helen began arithmetic next. Again she established the routine for recitation, instruction, practice, and the process to be used for students who completed their arithmetic to move on to the next subject.[20] She established her routines by following the course guides and by remembering what her teacher had done at the one-room school earlier in her young life.

During that morning, Helen began to discover which children were going to cooperate with her and which ones were going to test her. She remembered the older boys who had sat in the back of the room and smoked when she attended the one-room school. She hoped she wouldn't have that much trouble at Orion. So far, the children responded to a stern look or frown. She continued to work with them to establish the routines and expectations.

Lunchtime arrived. Helen had the children go by twos to get their lunch buckets. It was a nice day, so some of them went outside to eat and others settled down at their desks. The older girls gathered around Miss Helen's desk. All at once she felt very hungry. She also realized that she had not been to the bathroom. Miss Helen made a trip down the sandy path to the girl's outhouse and then returned to the lunch bucket that Mrs. Cossell had packed for her. It held a peanut-butter sandwich, an apple, and two cookies. Helen would find the same basic lunch for as long as she boarded with Mrs. Cossell. It certainly did taste good on this first day of school.

After eating lunch, Miss Helen and the older girls swept the schoolroom and began to plan ways they could make the room a little more attractive.[21] Soon the hour was gone and Miss Helen went to the doorway to ring the bell for the afternoon classes.

The afternoon went smoothly with only a few interruptions by the boys. Helen began to think that perhaps her concerns had been for nothing, because her pupils acted as though they were already into the routines. They went over grammar, geography, history, and physiology. Near the end of the day, she began the spelling lessons. She told the pupils they would have a spelling bee on Friday. At that point Louis began to gag and choke. He exclaimed, "Spelling makes me sick!"

Miss Helen decided to ignore the remark and continued to tell the children about the spelling bee. She assigned lists of words to each spelling group and told them to write the words down and begin studying. Louis continued to gag and moan, although it seemed like he was losing energy fast. Miss Helen continued to ignore him. Soon Louis was sitting quietly looking at his shoes. All of the other pupils were busy copying their lists of words.

At four o'clock, Helen announced that the pupils should put their books in their desks and prepare to go home. She sent them by rows to get their empty lunchbuckets and they were ready to go home. As had happened at noon, the older boys tumbled out of the door first, led by Louis. The younger girls left next and the older girls helped straighten the room and sweep the floor. Helen got her books together, for she would have to do a lot of outlining to stay ahead of the pupils.

The girls told Miss Helen good-bye and left. Helen took

one last look around the room, swished the dipper a couple of times and threw out the water that was remaining in the water bucket, and prepared to leave. She locked the door with the skeleton key, tucked the key in her bag, and began the two-mile walk back to Mrs. Cossell's house.

Her mind raced remembering all of the events of the day. She was pleased that most of the children seemed to like her and that they had been reasonably cooperative. She started thinking of the outlines she needed to prepare for the different groups in the different subjects. The two-mile distance did not seem long. As she turned into the driveway that led to Mrs. Cossell's house down to the canyon, Helen was pleased to smell the unmistakable odor of freshly baked bread. She was hungry.

She helloed to Mrs. Cossell as she entered the house. Mrs. Cossell was busy preparing supper in the lean-to kitchen. The boys were still doing chores, and Helen quickly changed out of her school dress. She welcomed this short period of privacy after coming home from school. She put her dress on a hanger, left it with her other school dresses on a nail in the wall at the end of her bed, changed into an old dress, and went to the kitchen to tell Mrs. Cossell about her day.

In no time at all, Mrs. Cossell had supper ready. She asked Helen to call the boys from the sheds. The smell of crispy fried chicken and gravy filled the air as Helen hurried out to tell the three boys that supper was ready. Helen had already washed up, and each boy used the washpan and soap that was on the back porch. They wiped on the long towel that hung on a nail nearby. The last one, usually the dirtiest, threw the soapy water out the back door onto the ground.

Suppertime conversation began with the boys asking about Helen's day. However, they soon interrupted her with stories of the previous schoolteacher and their own days at Orion School.

Darkness came early down in the canyon, and the flicker of the kerosene lanterns softened the harshness of the modest home and reflected the warm relationship between the Cossell boys and their mother. Helen was happy that she had been able to stay with the Cossells. They were certainly much poorer than her parents, but they seemed no poorer than the other people who lived in the Orion school district. The twenty dollars a month that she would pay would certainly help the family.

After supper, Helen worked on her outlines by lamplight. She worked until quite late that night to prepare the outlines she would put on the blackboard the next day for the children to copy. For the next few months, she would follow this same weeknight pattern.

The next morning, Helen ate breakfast quickly and hurried on to school. She wanted to get her outlines on the blackboard before the children arrived. As she unlocked the door and walked into the schoolroom, she realized that she would soon have to build a fire every morning to make the room comfortable for the children and for herself. She had put her outlines on the board and had prepared herself for the day by the time the first children arrived.

Miss Helen went to the door and rang her handbell to begin the day. It took a minute or two for the boys who were playing near the canyon to come into the room. Miss Helen noticed that the younger children had brought in all of the lunch pails and had put them in the cabinet.

After they saluted the flag, Miss Helen asked if someone would like to recite a poem or sing a song. Several children suggested that the Hedrick sisters could sing. After some protesting from the girls and some begging by the other children, the three older sisters—Helen, Lula, and Leota—

stood up and began to sing. Miss Helen was pleasantly surprised that the girls could really sing.

Thus started a morning opening exercise the pledge to the flag and a song from the Hedrick girls or some other type of entertainment. Helen believed this helped bring the children together and get them started in a positive way. Later in the year, she would take the Hedrick girls to other schools and to evening programs to perform. She was pleased to discover students who would be able to help her with the literary or evening programs she would have to plan as part of her responsibility.

After the morning exercises, Helen was happy as she looked around the room and saw all of the children working on their studies. Even Louis seemed to be applying himself to his work this morning.

At morning recess, Miss Helen went outside with the younger children. They showed her, over the edge of the canyon, where the path to the Cossell home and the road intersected. She resolved to follow the path that evening. As she went back into the school to ring the bell, she noticed that the children had a very poor place to play. There was no designated playground or fence. Children could wander as far as they wished as long as they still could hear the bell.[22] She decided to help organize some games at lunchtime.

As the children worked on their assignments, Helen poked about the room. In the back of the old cupboard she found an old volleyball net and a slightly flat ball. This would be the lunchtime activity, she decided. She enjoyed playing games and knew that playing volleyball with the children would be fun.

After everyone had eaten lunch, Miss Helen announced to the older girls, who again stayed inside with her, that they were going to play volleyball. They were a little surprised, but went outside to find two sticks to hold up the net. Miss Helen carried the old ball outside and went to the small children to ask who wanted to play. The little boys squealed with excitement and ran over to the older boys at the edge of the canyon. Soon all of the pupils were gathered around. The girls had managed to tie the net to some long branches and had agreed among themselves that two people would have to take turns holding up the net. Miss Helen helped divide the children into two fairly matched groups, with Louis, who was as tall as she, on one side and herself on the other.

They had a wonderful time! The sand was deep and it was impossible to keep boundaries marked, but they enjoyed batting the ball back and forth. Helen, although not athletic, always enjoyed outside activities. The children were delighted that Miss Helen had joined in the game. As lunchtime drew to a close, she noticed Louis's eyes on her. That look reminded her of the glances she had sometimes received from the farmhands as she had worked in the fields with them and her father. This seemed to be another problem to deal with, she thought, and went in to ring the bell.

As the children entered the schoolroom, two of the boys agreed to find some good poles for the volleyball net, and another agreed to bring a tire pump to inflate the ball. As the year went on, the students enjoyed volleyball, Annie-over, blackman, and other organized games. Helen tried to play with the children as often as she could while the weather was nice.

Again that afternoon Helen noticed that Louis's eyes were often on her. She hoped that if she just ignored him, he would stop looking at her that way. Near the end of the day, she told the children they needed to begin thinking about a box supper sometime in September. She asked them to talk to their parents that evening and said they would begin to plan the program the next day.

Four o'clock came. The children were dismissed, and Helen prepared to leave. She erased the blackboard and washed it with the water left in the drinking-water bucket. She swept the floor, although the girls had already swept it. She locked the door and went over to the place on the road where the path came out of the canyon. She hoped that she wouldn't get lost as she started down the path into the canyon. The path was clear, as many children had used it over the years. The path was also used by game as the animals moved up and down the canyon. Although there was no water, the sandy path showed that when the rains and snows came, water would also use that path through the canyon.

Helen noticed the difference in temperature and lack of wind right away. She could hear the wind in the trees along the rim of the canyon and yet it was very quiet on the path. She saw the tracks of deer, quail, wild turkeys, coyotes, and rabbits. In the trees overhead she could hear the birds settling for the night. The walk home seemed much shorter. She would use this path as often as she could.

The days flew. Soon it was Friday of the first week. John would pick Helen up right after school. The pupils ended their day with a spelling bee. Helen was pleased that the children had learned their words so well. Some of the girls stayed a few minutes to help her clean the schoolroom before the weekend, and Helen was able to leave in record time. By the time she arrived at Mrs. Cossell's, her father's truck was waiting for her. He was inside talking to Mrs. Cossell and her oldest son. They were laughing and swapping stories as Helen arrived. She gave her dad a big hug, kissed him, and grabbed her bag of dirty clothes and the books she would need for the weekend. Helen told Mrs.

Cossell she would be back Sunday evening, then left with her father.

Helen chatted about the children in her school all the way to Seiling. John laughed and asked if she had missed her own family during the week she had been gone. Helen leaned over and gave her dad a big hug to assure him that she had not forgotten him.

The weekend went quickly, and Helen enjoyed telling her mother and little sister all about the children. She had to wash and iron her clothes, and she enjoyed the luxury of a hot bath in a real tub. The Hussmans did not have running water but did have a bathtub in which they could pour water heated on the stove. The tub drained out into the garden; water could not be wasted in western Oklahoma. At the Cossell's, Helen was able to take only sponge bathes after the boys had gone to bed. She worked on her school things a little but enjoyed seeing her friend at the community dance on Saturday night.

After one of Stella's big Sunday dinners, John took Helen back to the Cossells'. And so began another routine. John would pick Helen up on Friday afternoon and take her back on Sunday evening or on Monday morning.

John often needed Helen's help with farm chores on the weekends. At hog-butchering time, John had the water boiling when he returned home with her. After shooting the hog between the eyes, he tied a rope to its hind feet and he and Helen used a pulley on a beam above the barrel to raise the hog over the boiling water. Then, as Helen guided the hog, he lowered it slowly into the water. They pulled it up together and again John lowered it into the water, scalding it carefully. Together, he and Helen scraped the hog and cut it up.

At Orion the children were busy planning for a box supper at the end of September. Helen had seen a number of things she wanted to buy for the school and the box supper would help raise money for them. She had checked with Mrs. Cossell, who worked with the other schoolboard members to approve the date for the event. The children told their parents, and notices were posted at the post office at Orion Store and at Bado Store, the location of the nearest telephone.

The Hedrick girls were practicing their songs. Other pupils were busy decorating the room for the event. The younger children drew pictures to hang on the walls, and the older girls made a calendar on a portion of the blackboard, using colored chalk. They worked very hard to decorate it for the month of September. There weren't many colors left in the chalk box, and the box supper could help buy another box.

One morning when Helen opened the schoolroom, she knew she would need to start a fire to ward off the chill. She went outside to find some starter wood. There were a few small branches behind the girls' outhouse; the boys had probably been using them to scratch on the walls to scare the girls, Helen thought. She noticed that the new wood supply for the year had been placed near the school. As she picked up several small logs, she realized that she would need to organize the children to help her get kindling wood and bring it in.

Helen started the fire with some paper and the branches that she had found. The old stove worked quite well, and soon the chill was gone. During her years of teaching, making the morning fire became Helen's least-favorite task; however, it was essential that the schoolroom be warm by the time that the children arrived.

The weather continued to be fairly mild through September. Helen played outside with her pupils as much as she could. Louis was becoming a bigger problem with each passing day. He encouraged the other boys to be late coming in from lunch, laughed at the children who did not do well in recitation, and often pretended not to hear Miss Helen as she asked him to recite. It was becoming more and more difficult for her to discipline the other pupils when they saw him misbehaving.

One day as Miss Helen was on the playground watching the small children play a game, she became aware of Louis standing behind her. She turned around and he began to tell her how attractive he thought she was. He told her that he had "lots of experience" and could show her a "real good time" if she would go out with him. Helen looked at him coldly and, without saying a word, returned to the schoolroom. Her heart was pounding and her knees were shaking. She wondered what she was supposed to do next.

Miss Helen rang the bell and went on with the afternoon activities. She wondered what Louis had told the other boys. She noticed that they had come in with Louis and that they had been awfully quiet. Several times that afternoon Louis had spoken out, made fun of the other children, and challenged Miss Helen's directions.

That evening Helen talked to Mrs. Cossell about Louis. Mrs. Cossell said she was surprised that Helen had gotten along with him as well as she had. She said the school board had met with his father the previous year because Louis was so unruly. They had warned him that Louis would not be able to stay in school if he continued to misbehave. She told Helen that the school board would meet with his parents during the next week and warn them again. If things didn't improve, Louis would not be allowed to attend Orion School.[23]

Helen managed to keep the children busy and made sure she was not alone with Louis. Within a few days, the word was around that Louis and his parents would have to meet with the school board. All of the mischief ended quickly. The older boys turned their energies toward their studies and getting ready for the box supper.

On the day of the supper, Helen and the children spent all afternoon cleaning and arranging the schoolroom. They even washed the windows and took the curtains outside to air. They went through the program, with the younger children reciting a poem, the Hedrick girls singing, and one of the older boys reading an essay. Helen had arranged for a friend of her father to be the auctioneer. Stella and Donna were bringing boxes, and Helen just hoped the community would come. She had borrowed lamps to light the schoolroom and had three buckets of fresh water for the patrons to drink with their meals.

There was very little reason for Helen to worry. The school was filled, the children did well in their program, and, although the boxes did not bring as much as those at Seiling, the profits were eighteen dollars—as much as Orion School had ever earned. The community seemed very happy with its new teacher.

On the last Friday of September, Helen received her first pay as a teacher: a warrant from the Orion school board for eighty dollars. She took it to the bank in Seiling and got twenty dollars to pay Mrs. Cossell and ten dollars for spending money. She put the remainder in her savings account. This would become her pattern. She had learned to be very frugal.

The next few weeks flew by. The children seemed to be intent upon learning the materials presented. The seventh- and eighth-graders were busily copying the outlines in their notebooks to prepare for the county examinations. The beginners were actually starting to learn to read and were always ready for their recitation time. Helen had enjoyed describing her students to her mentor, Mable, when she saw her in Seiling on some weekends. Whenever Helen had a question or a problem, she could always count on Mable to give her advice or suggestions.

The children at Orion were busy thinking about Halloween. The school Halloween party was always a big event for the entire family. After the success of the box supper, more children were willing to take part in the next program. The Hedrick girls were learning new songs, and several children were learning verses of poetry, but the most fun of all was planning for the party. They would get a washtub and bob for apples. Helen had a friend in Seiling who was good at telling ghost stories; she agreed to dress up as a witch and come to the school that evening. They planned some activities for children too young to be in school. Some of the money from the box supper was spent for colored paper, scissors, glue, colored chalk, and other materials needed to decorate the room. Helen kept the proceeds from the fund-raiser in her bank account and submitted an accounting to the school board once a month.

In the midst of planning the Halloween party, Helen learned in a newletter from the county superintendent's office that she was to attend the first regional teachers' meeting held at the normal school in Alva. She arranged to ride up to the Saturday meeting with her friend Twila Donnelly, who taught at Richmond, a school just west of Seiling. They stayed all night with Twila's cousin Bertha, who lived in Alva. After the meeting, they went to eat supper at Nall's Café, a popular gathering place for college students. As they sat down at a table, Bertha pointed to a table of boys who were wearing letter sweaters and showed them the one she wanted to go with. Helen and Twila looked him over. Bertha said his name was Lon Morris and he played football. He was tall and muscular and was talking a great deal to the others at the table. Helen thought the way he smoked his cigarette and gestured as he talked was pretty cocky, but she didn't see anyone who looked any more interesting.

When they finished their meal, the three girls went back to Bertha's and talked far into the night: about their schools, their weekend activities, and boys. Twila planned to continue attending summer sessions at Alva, and she was interested in finding out about eligible males. Helen was interested in learning more about Alva, too, for she would be starting classes in the next spring session to meet the requirements for recertification.

It was a very special weekend for Helen. She had gotten a taste of a very different life, and she liked it very much. She looked forward to the beginning of college. She didn't go back to Orion until Monday morning because she wanted to tell her parents and Donna about her trip to Alva.

As Helen helped the children prepare for their Halloween party, her thoughts sometimes returned to the college campus and the fun the students seemed to be having. However, she conducted her classes as usual and soon was looking forward to the party.

On the evening of the party, community routines changed considerably. Everyone had to come to the party in costume. Rugged farmhands who worked hard all day for very little pay joined their excited children in putting on some type of disguise. They put lamp soot on their faces, or women's bonnets and lipstick, or pressed wet coffee grounds to their faces to resemble stubbly beards. Everyone was excited about dressing up and going to the party.

Helen arranged for some community members to bring buckets of milk and for others to bring tin cups. She got chocolate and sugar from her mother and made hot chocolate on the woodstove. The room was lighted by kerosene lamps brought by some of the patrons.

Helen was particularly excited about the storytelling

part of the program. She and her friend the storyteller asked Mrs. Cossell to help them with the props that they needed. They put the entrails from several chickens into a big bowl. They had everyone sit down to listen, and as the storyteller got to a certain place, Helen turned out the last lamp and it was pitch black in the schoolroom. The guests were told to reach into the bowl as it came around. Just as they expected and hoped, everybody squealed and hollered as they felt the cold, slimy mess. They all had a wonderful time. The Halloween party was a rousing success.

One weekend in early November, Mable asked Helen whether she planned to go to the state teachers' meeting in Oklahoma City. Although Helen told her she hadn't heard anything about such a meeting, Mable informed her that all teachers in the state were required to attend. Helen quickly asked if she could go with Mable, and they planned the trip.

As the time for the meeting approached, Helen began to get excited. She would enjoy the chance to meet other teachers, but most of all she looked forward to getting some new ideas for teaching her children. Helen and Mable and several other teachers from their area went to the meeting together. They saw all kinds of teaching equipment and materials on display in the exhibit area; however, the speakers were a real disappointment to Helen. None of them talked about how a rural teacher could teach seven or eight subjects in eight grades all at the same time. Helen was quiet on the way back to Seiling. The only people she had met so far who seemed to know what she was trying to deal with were other rural teachers like Mable. She was so glad that Mable was her friend.

Not everything was perfect in Helen's schoolroom. Louis was much more cooperative, but he was absent a lot. Some of the other children had begun to misbehave. Miss Helen's stern look usually resulted in the pupils' getting quiet or stopping whatever it was they were doing that they were not supposed to be doing. Sometimes she had pupils who had misbehaved stay in for recess, and sometimes she had them "stand on the floor." She remembered a time when she had been in the fourth grade and her teacher made her stand on the floor. As Helen stood on the raised platform near the teacher's desk with her back to the class and her book in her hands, her book got heavier and heavier. She stood first on one foot and then on the other. She remembered thinking that the teacher would never let her sit down again. Helen tried not to use these punishments with her pupils very often.

The pupils had told her about the punishments used by the previous teachers: spanking with a yardstick, ruler, or switch; standing in the corner; standing with the pupil's nose in a circle on the blackboard; staying under the teacher's desk; and standing on the floor. Helen was glad that the children seemed to respond to her scolding and that she rarely had to punish anyone.

One day, however, one of the beginners refused to be quiet, regardless of the looks or the scolding, and Helen kept him in during recess. After the other children had left the room, she walked over to his desk and started to talk to him about his misbehavior. The little tyke looked up at his teacher with fury in his eyes and said, "You old tunk!"

Miss Helen knew he had a speech problem and had meant to call her an "old skunk." She stifled her urge to laugh and also her urge to become even angrier with him. She calmly told him to put his head down and to sit in his seat until the other children came back from recess. He behaved much better the rest of the afternoon.

The weather started to get very cold. The north wind blowing across the plains could chill a person to the bone. The distance that many of the children had to walk became a real problem in the cold. Mr. Estes fixed a one-horse cart for his three children to ride the two and a half miles to school. The cart had two wheels and would tilt back onto the ground as soon as the horse was unhitched. Mr. Estes had put a board across the cart for the children's seat. Luther, who was twelve years old, could hook up the horse and cart and drive his little sister Alveretta and little brother Claude to and from school. While they were at school, Luther tied the horse to a tree and filled an old bucket with water from the cistern. During recess and at lunchtime, Luther and some of the older boys walked the horse and sometimes took short bareback rides, if no one told the teacher.

The Hedrick children also had to walk two and a half miles to school. Often the girls would walk one-half mile east and hitch a ride with the Estes children in the cart. One morning when the weather was not too cold, Luther stopped to pick up the Hedrick girls. The seven children were giggling and squirming in the cart when Luther saw something jump up out of the grass. The horse reared, turning the cart over. The children all tumbled out of the cart onto the sandy road. As the horse struggled to get loose from the cart, he broke the cart's shaft. The Hedrick girl's brother Willie, who had jumped out of the grass, came over at once to help straighten out the mess he had created. He and Luther unhitched the horse and walked back to the Estes farm to face Luther's father. The four girls and Claude walked on to school, filled with the story of what had happened to them on the way to school. They felt lucky that no one had been hurt.

Although Willie maintained that he had been waiting for the others and had just raised up when he heard the horse and cart, the others believed he had intended to scare them. Mr. Estes fixed the cart, but cautioned Luther that he was to take only his own brother and sister in it from then on.

The long walk facing the north wind was very cold for the Hedrick girls. One of the school-board members who was single lived close to the route the girls took to school. They would often hear his car starting as they approached, and he would give them a ride to school. In addition to their good singing voices, the girls were also very pretty and their older sister was still single. Although he never said anything directly, the girls suspected that the bachelor wanted them to put in a good word for him with their sister. They were very glad to get a ride but left him on his own with their sister.

One morning when it was very cold, the girls decided to take a shortcut across an open wheatfield. The farther they walked, the colder the sharp north wind seemed to get. The littler sister, Leora, began to cry. The older Hedrick girls, Helen, Lula, and Leota, encouraged her to keep following them. They scolded her for being such a baby as they stumbled against the wind, which pulled and tore at their coats and the scarves that wrapped their heads. Finally they reached a windbreak between the field and a pasture. As they tried to warm their hands and feet before going on to school, little Leora began to laugh. Concerned that she had gone loco, Lula, Helen, and Leota ran to her at once. Leora told them her tears had frozen on her eyelashes and she could now see a beautiful rainbow sight in the sunshine.

When they got to school, Miss Helen had the fire going and the schoolroom warm. During the harsh winter, Miss Helen wore high leather lace-up boots and a heavy raincoat with a hood as she walked up the canyon path to school. She was glad she could use the path through the canyon, especially on the very cold mornings. Many children wore overshoes even when it was not snowing or raining so they could keep their feet warmer.

In winter the schoolroom was not a very pleasant place, as can be seen in this passage from *America's Country Schools:* "The smells of wet wool clothes and bags of asafetida, an offensive-smelling resinous material hung around children's necks as health amulets, drove many teachers to open the windows, only to be met by a blast of icy wind. As soon as the window was closed, the air again became stuffy. Students alternately froze and roasted, depending on their proximity to the potbellied stove. The corners of the room could be almost as cold as the out-of-doors. The constant freezing and thawing of the children's feet gave them chilblains, which made their feet itch intensely as they warmed up, so that throughout the day, the room resounded with the constant noise of boots shuffling under the desks."[24]

Helen and the children were busily planning their Thanksgiving program. More and more of the children were volunteering to take part in the programs. They decorated the schoolroom with paper turkeys and scenes from their history books and decided to ask some parents to bring cookies to have with the hot chocolate for refreshments. Helen was encouraged by the enthusiasm of the children and their parents.

It was so cold outside that they began more inside activities during recess and lunchtime. They would dash outside to the outhouses, but only the heartiest of the older boys stayed outside. Because the girls were very interested in their appearance and because Miss Helen went to Seiling every weekend and attended lots of social activities, the girls were very interested in her clothes and her hairdo. Lula Hedrick had learned to do finger waves from her older sister. Often after they had eaten lunch, Miss Helen and Lula would fix the girls' hair. The boys would make fun of them, but the girls enjoyed trying out new looks. Helen suspected that the wool hats and scarves and the long walks home managed to disturb any change in hairstyle by the time the girls got home.

Once Helen had finished the outlines, she began to enjoy her evenings with Mrs. Cossell. Helen joined her in starting to piece a quilt and also started to embroider a pillow with a view of a pine tree and little log cabin that reminded her of the Cossell's house. They would sometimes take the Cossells' Model T touring car to neighbors' homes for card parties during the week. Helen heard about the dances that were held at the Holubs' on weekends, but she was not able to attend because her father continued to pick her up on Friday evenings.

The roads were very poor and the Model T frequently got stuck in the sand. Many times Helen would take the wheel as her father pushed the truck out of the sand. Although the nearest telephone was seven miles from the school at Bado, the mailman from Orion Store came by the school every day. He would often get stuck as he tried to make it up the sandy hill by the school. When they heard the familiar sound of wheels spinning in the sand, Miss Helen would give the pupils permission to run out and push the mailman's Model T up the hill.

Thanksgiving came and went, and the school program at Orion was a success. Although no one said anything to Helen about her work, she felt that she was doing a good job. She had heard that if a teacher was not doing well, the school board would contact the county superintendent and he would make a special visit to the school.

Helen began to think about Christmas. She knew she wanted to have a big party at the school, with a Christmas tree and lots of decorations, but she also wanted to do something very special for the children. One weekend she talked to her dad about planning something special. John had been to the livestock markets in Enid and had heard the town was planning a big parade on the Saturday before Christmas. He suggested that he drive the grain truck and take the children to the Santa Claus parade in Enid. It was a wonderful idea! Helen could hardly wait to tell the children on Monday morning.

As Helen expected, the children were very excited. Few of them had been the twenty-eight miles to Fairview, the county seat, and none had made the seventy-mile trip to Enid, the largest town in the region. She told them to go home and ask if their parents would allow them to go with Mr. and Mrs. Hussman and Miss Helen. The parents were as enthusiastic as their children, so the trip was planned.

Helen also contacted the grocer in Seiling, who gave teachers a special price on treats for their pupils. She ordered sacks of candy, nuts, and fruit that she would give the children at the Christmas party. She also let the pupils draw names for presents, with a ten-cent limit on price.

During lunchtimes in December, Miss Helen and her pupils began to decorate the schoolroom for Christmas. They cut out snowflakes for the windows and began to make decorations for the tree. They knew they could not put candles on the tree, but they could make lots of decorations out of colored paper, popcorn, and berries. On the Friday before the trip to Enid, Miss Helen and the children went down into the canyon to cut a Christmas tree. After much discussion, they finally chose a well-shaped cedar tree. The older boys took turns chopping with the ax. They then pulled the tree back up out of the canyon to the schoolhouse and put it in a bucket of wet sand.

Lessons were put aside that afternoon and they decorated the tree. Everyone agreed that after they finished it was the most beautiful tree they had ever seen. Miss Helen reminded the pupils to be at the school early the next morning with warm clothes and their lunches for the trip to Enid.

Helen, Stella, and John arrived at Orion School early the next morning and found that most of the children were already waiting for them. A few of the parents brought their children to see them off. Several little children who had not yet started school were also being sent along on the outing. John had filled the truck bed with clean straw, and Stella had brought all of her extra quilts. Miss Helen got into the back of the truck with the children, and the little ones immediately curled up next to her. They covered up with the quilts and everyone waved to the parents in the school-yard as John started toward Enid.

The sun was shining but the wind was very cold. At first the children sang Christmas carols; however, they were soon burrowed under the quilts, excitedly anticipating what they were going to see in Enid. After they passed through Fairview, the land flattened out and there was not much to be seen from the road. The truck was running well and the roads were good. The hum of the wheels on the hard-surfaced road lulled most of the children to sleep. As Miss Helen started to doze, one of the children pulled on her arm. She said her little brother was crying and wouldn't tell her why. Miss Helen, thinking he was cold, tried to pull him toward her. He pulled away and began to cry even more. Miss Helen didn't know what to do, for he was a little tyke and not yet in school. She rapped on the window of the cab to get her dad's attention. John stopped the truck and came around to the back of the truck. Miss Helen pointed out the little boy who was crying and explained that she didn't know why.

John went over and picked him up over the side of the

truck. The little boy whispered in John's ear. John smiled, put him down on the ground beside the truck to do his duty, and said to the other children, "Okay, do any of the rest of you need to go to the bathroom?" The children laughed and shook their heads. Miss Helen breathed a sigh of relief as John hoisted the little boy back into the truck. She tucked the quilts around the children, and John pulled the truck back onto the road toward Enid.

When they passed the road to Lahoma, where her grandparents lived, Miss Helen began to wake the children. It was only twelve more miles, and the started a game of trying to be the first to see Enid as they approached it across the flat countryside. It was decided that there was no clear winner, because several of the children shouted at the same time when they saw the signs of the town as they approached. John found a parking place on the square in the center of town, and Miss Helen began organizing the eating of lunches. Some of the children wanted to stay in the warm truck bed to eat and others decided to get out and eat on the picnic benches in the park, which made up the two-block square surrounding the post office and the Garfield County courthouse. Although the Major County courthouse was similar, most of the children had not seen buildings this large or impressive. They were able to use the public facilities, and everyone seemed content and happy.

Soon it was time for the parade to start. The parade route passed around the entire square, so they had a good place from which to watch. There were bands, horses, and bicycles. The children marveled at the colors and also the number of people who were watching. They had never seen that many people in one place before. Local dignitaries rode by in open cars, and finally the main attraction could be seen. In a wagon made to look like a sleigh pulled by real reindeer were Mr. and Mrs. Claus. Helen caught her breath.

This was the first large parade she had watched, and she had never before seen anything so beautiful. Santa Claus had on a bright-red velvet suit with white fur trim, and Mrs. Claus was wearing a beautiful white velvet dress with white fur trim. Helen could not take her eyes off the sight, although she could hear the oohs and aahs of those around her. As the sleigh pulled out of sight, Santa's helpers came by, giving bags of candies, nuts, and fruits to the children in the crowd. What a special day for all of them!

Helen ran over and threw her arms around her father. "Thank you for bringing us!" she cried. She felt like a child herself as her pupils echoed her thanks.

John threw back his head and laughed. "I have had a lot of fun too," he told them. After making sure that everyone had been to the bathroom, the Hussmans loaded the children into the truck for the trip home. Many of the children had begun to eat their favorite goodies out of the treat sacks. The way home seemed much shorter. Helen could not forget the beautiful sight of Mr. and Mrs. Claus in their sleigh.

It was dark when they reached the Orion community. John drove down the roads, letting children out as close to their homes as possible. "Oh, thank you, Mr. Hussman!" rang out at each stop as children left the truck and scampered home. It was a very happy family who drove to the Hussman farm that night.

The next week the children put on the Christmas program at Orion School. They had their gift exchange, and Miss Helen gave them her treats. The parents brought lots of cookies, cakes, and other goodies to share. John and Stella attended the party. The parents crowded around them and thanked them for the trip to the Enid parade. Helen went home with her parents to celebrate Christmas with her family. She also celebrated her twentieth birthday on New Year's Day 1930.

Shortly after Christmas, Helen received a notice of a county teachers' meeting to be held at Fairview. She contacted Mable and they planned to attend together. Mable asked Helen if Mr. Weaver had been to visit her school yet. When Helen reported that he had not yet come, Mable told her that she must be doing all right then. At the teachers' meeting, Mr. Weaver reminded the teachers about the records that they should be keeping and about the new curriculum guides that were being written. He asked whether everyone was receiving the monthly newsletter from his office. Helen felt a little sorry for the superintendent because he seemed to be so proud of the newsletter, and yet she had not found it to be particularly helpful to her.

At a break in the meeting, Helen went to a small book publishers' display. She looked at all of the library and reference books that were there and thought about the few old and torn books her pupils called their library. Helen decided to buy *The Library of Knowledge,* "a compact, comprehensive storehouse of general knowledge treating history, geography, biography, literature, economics, civics, art, science, discovery, and invention, embracing over 16,000 subjects." She paid $37.50 of her own money for the five-volume set. She felt that it would be a welcome addition to her schoolroom and she had been saving her money. She placed her order for the books, which would be delivered by mail in several weeks, and tried to imagine how excited the children would be when they arrived.

Once again Helen was disappointed that what happened at the meeting didn't seem to help her become a better teacher. She did enjoy seeing the other teachers and liked catching up on the gossip. The meeting had reminded her of the importance of upcoming examinations and the need to make sure that her pupils were adequately prepared to pass them. She felt good that she had been able to keep the children up with the time lines in the curriculum guides. However, she knew that the hardest time lay ahead. Her school had a term of only 160 days, so she would have to work hard with the children, who had to compete with children who had school terms of 180 days.[25]

When Helen returned to her school, she began to plan very carefully how she would prepare her seventh- and eighth-graders for the county examinations. The first chance to pass them would be in April, the second in May. She placed the examination dates on the chalkboard as a reminder.

The holiday for January was Temperance Day. The new state law[26] said that all schools must observe it on the Friday nearest the 16th day of January. The state superintendent's office had sent out a program to be covered on that day in every school in Oklahoma. It included the history of the Temperance movement and the physiological values of temperance. Helen planned to use the materials during physiology class. The weather was very stormy, and she decided not to plan an evening program during January.

Helen and the Cossells stayed close to home on evenings when the weather was bad. They often played cards after supper, and Helen made good progress on her quilt top and pillow. She had begun to be very fond of the oldest Cossell boy, Millard. Their relationship developed like the one she had with her cousin Fred, who had come from Iowa to work on the farm, but Helen wondered whether something else might develop for them.

The days and weeks went quickly. Helen continued to get her warrant for eighty dollars at the end of each month and was always able to cash it at the bank at Seiling. However, she had heard about some teachers who were having trouble cashing their warrants, because the school boards were having trouble collecting their taxes and therefore had no money in their bank accounts. Helen was relieved that she was not having that kind of trouble.

One morning in late January as the pupils were beginning their first recitations, they heard a car stop outside the school. Some of the children ran to the window to see who had come. One of the older students announced that it was the county superintendent. The children knew he came to their school each year for a visit. Miss Helen knew the county superintendents came to the schools to see how well the teacher did with the pupils. She knew he would want to hear the children recite. She had heard that some areas of the state had teacher supervisors who came to the schools to help teachers.[27] However, the county superintendent did not really have time to help teachers. His job included many more responsibilities than he could possibly handle alone, and yet little, if any, assistance was offered in Major County. There were 112 dependent schools in the county which had to be supervised by the superintendent that year.

The recitations went very well; the children were on their very best behavior and stood tall and proud as they recited their lessons. The older pupils copied studiously in their notebooks from material on the blackboard. Helen noticed that Mr. Weaver made notes as he walked around the room. At recess the children all ran out into the cold, whooping and hollering as they used some of their pent-up energy. Mr. Weaver asked Helen about the curriculum and how many children she had who would have to take the county examinations. She informed him that she would have three and possibly four, if Louis returned. Soon it was time to call the children in with her bell. She thought Mr. Weaver looked pleased as they settled down to work immediately. Just before noon, Mr. Weaver walked out of the schoolhouse. The children continued their work, but she could hear a big sigh of relief. The superintendent walked around the school building and to the outhouses before getting into his car and driving away. Miss Helen would not see the superintendent in her school again until the next year when he made his annual visit, nor would she ever know what he had written in his notes.[28] As they heard Mr. Weaver's car start, Miss Helen announced that it was time for lunch.

Helen was glad that nothing terrible had happened during the superintendent's visit. One of the horror stories told by teachers had to do with a county superintendent's visit to a new teacher. The superintendent asked her class who discovered America. There was silence as the children, with long faces, looked down at their feet. The new teacher was horrified. Finally one little boy cautiously put up his hand and the superintendent, breathing a sigh of relief, called on him. The boy said with a shy smile, "Twern't Bill Murray, twer it?"[29]. The teachers always laughed at the story, but they secretly feared such an event in their own schools.

The month of February brought Valentine's Day and the celebration of Washington's and Lincoln's birthdays. On a weekend visit with her grandparents, Helen had seen some Valentine cards in her Grandpa Sterba's old store. She wanted to give her pupils something nice, so she bought one for each of them. She also bought some white paper lace and red paper so that the children could made Valentines for one another.

There were several snowstorms that month, making it difficult for students and their teacher to get to school. When the snow was deep, Helen would have to walk to school on the road; the canyon path was impassable in deep snow.

One day in early February, the mailman stopped with a big box for Miss Helen. The pupils knew immediately that it had to contain books. It was *The Library of Knowledge* that Miss Helen had ordered. Everyone was very excited to see what was inside. They had strict rules about using the new books. The older children would make sure that their hands were clean, and they would turn the pages for the little ones. None of the children had seen such big, beautiful books as these, with their embossed green leather covers and gold lettering. It was a privilege to get to look up an answer to a question in *The Library of Knowledge.* At the end of the day, Helen sat and looked at the books she had bought. As she carefully turned the pages, she thought, "This is almost like having a real library."

The children planned a program for Washington's Birthday. They decided to have a pie supper along with their entertainment, because their school supplies were getting pretty low and the money they could make from the sale of pies could carry them to the end of school. Miss Helen knew that she would have to spend much of her energy in the next few months getting the pupils ready for the county examinations. She knew her reputation as a teacher and her chances for being hired for the second year depended on the scores her pupils made on the examinations.

The children decided to put on a patriotic play in honor of George Washington. They used information from their history book as well as the new encyclopedias and wrote a play called *The Father of Our Country.* The Hedrick girls practiced singing "America the Beautiful." Miss Helen hoped some of the people would bring cherry pies in keeping with the theme of the event. She also hoped it would not snow that night.

Miss Helen brought some men's coats and hats and some long skirts as costumes for the play. Alveretta decided to borrow her mother's reading glasses to make her look older for her part. The children and the teacher enjoyed preparing for the program.

It was cold but clear on the night of the February program. Helen's parents brought their neighbors, and Donna, of course, from Seiling. Helen was happy to see that two of the three pies they brought were cherry. She had made a big pot of coffee and another of hot chocolate and had them simmering on the stove as the guests arrived. The schoolroom was decorated with a mixture of red and white valentines and patriotic pictures and sayings. Donna helped her sister arrange the pies and the tin plates, cups, and forks they would use after the program.

Soon the room was filled with people. From grandmothers to babies, everyone came to the school programs. The Orion community did not have a post office or even a store. As was true throughout rural America, the school was what held the community together and made it a community. The schoolteacher had a serious responsibility not only to the pupils but also to the community. The Hedrick girls sang beautifully and the play went well. Some of the older boys laughed when Alveretta couldn't read her part with the glasses on, and when she put them on the end of her nose so that she could see over them, they fell to the floor. The community did not seem to mind the altering of history when Abraham Lincoln appeared in a scene with George Washington. The applause was long and loud at the end of the play.

The guests paid ten cents each for a slice of pie and a hot drink. Miss Helen collected the money in a little tin box, which she carefully placed in the bottom of her book bag. She would ride home with the Cossells after everyone left. She had heard stories of teachers who had been robbed as they walked home from fund-raisers, and she hoped the hard times would not affect the people around Orion in that way.

At the end of February, Miss Helen and the seventh-

and eighth-graders began to get very serious about preparation for the examinations. The last newsletter from Mr. Weaver had said the pupils in schools with fewer than five children taking the examinations would have to go to Fairview on April 18 to take the tests. Miss Helen had five children who could take the examinations if she counted Louis. However, he had stopped coming to school regularly and she doubted the he could pass them anyway. So she began to plan tutoring sessions for three of the Hedrick children—Willie, Lula, and Helen—and for Luther Estes. The two boys had to take the eighth-grade examinations and all of the subjects they had not passed when they took the seventh-grade examinations. Lula had to take the seventh-grade ones, and Helen was to take the examination in Oklahoma history offered to sixth-graders. Of course, Miss Helen had to continue teaching the rest of her pupils as she began to prepare the four for their examinations. They continued with their routines of recitation, drill work, and practice and looked forward to the Friday-afternoon spelling bees.

In March the weather improved significantly. Miss Helen noticed the early spring flowers thrusting their showy heads through the snow that remained in the shadows along the canyon path. She watched for signs of newborn rabbits. In addition to preparing her pupils for the examinations and teaching her classes, she had to plan an Arbor Day program for the Friday after the first Monday in March. The blackjack oak trees that grew in clumps not far from the schoolhouse didn't seem like much to celebrate. Miss Helen wondered how she was supposed to follow the directions sent down from the state legislature.[30] She thought she might bring some small evergreen trees up from the canyon and plant them near the school. "But who would water them during the long and dry Oklahoma summer?" she thought. Miss

Helen sighed and wondered whether the people making all of those regulations had any idea about the things she had to do and how little help she had. Anyway, there would have to be some kind of Arbor Day exercise. Since it was nearly time to plant gardens, perhaps they could talk about planting seeds and taking care of plants instead of just trees.

One March evening Mrs. Cossell told Helen the school board had met and had decided to ask Helen to stay another year at Orion. She told Helen that everyone was pleased with her. Helen was very excited. She was doing a good job, and she had her school for another year.

Miss Helen planned to stay at Mrs. Cossell's the three Saturdays before the county examinations. She would use the extra days to drill her pupils. Miss Helen put on the board the name of each pupil and what he or she had to study. They diligently made their notebooks for the subjects in which they would be tested. If for some reason they were missing part of a notebook, they would copy from another pupil's or from the teacher's. Luther had to take tests in ten areas. He had missed some school and was behind in some of his subjects. His little sister Alveretta tried to help by copying some of the outlines for him. Willie had passed some of his subjects the year before; therefore, he had to study for only four subjects. Lula had to take tests in four areas, and Helen would take only one.

To prepare the pupils, Miss Helen quizzed them on the various subjects. They all worked together on Oklahoma history because they all had to take that test. Helen Hedrick helped her brother and sister drill for physiology and hygiene, geography, and arithmetic. The boys studied together for agriculture, the girls for domestic science. Frequently during the week, all of the children in the class would join in the drills for the examinations. The little ones knew that they, too, would have to take the county examinations someday. By hearing the lessons many times, the children learned from one another.[31]

The Saturdays at Orion were not all work. At last Helen got to go to the dances at the Holubs' and to a couple of parties with Millard Cossell. She enjoyed being a part of the community outside the school.

She arranged to borrow her father's 1925 Model T Ford coupé to take the children to the examination in Fairview. The superintendent held it on a Saturday to keep from interrupting the rest of the children's schooling. His office was always open on Saturday anyway.[32] Miss Helen drilled the children all the way to Fairview, hoping they would not be too nervous to show what they had learned.

During the examinations, each teacher was assigned to monitor students she did not teach. Helen worked with children she did not know. At the end of the long, hard day her own pupils piled back into the car to go home. The ride home was much quieter than the one to Fairview. They were all exhausted from the tension and the long day of taking tests.

The children received the results of their examinations through the mail several weeks later. To Helen's pride and relief, Luther passed all of his and Willie passed all of his, although he made a score of only 60 percent in physiology. Lula did not pass domestic science and would have to take it again with the rest of her examinations the following year. Helen had 84 percent in Oklahoma history and was proud of her high score. Miss Helen could feel proud and secure in her job as a result of the test scores.

The end of the school year was approaching rapidly. The warmer weather invited some visitors into the schoolroom. Sometimes during recitation, pupils in the back of the room would become very noisy. Miss Helen would ask, "What's the matter back there?" The children would reply,

"There's a snake in here!" Miss Helen would grab the broom that was near her desk and run back to chase the snake out the door. She would try to kill it if it were a rattler.

As they began to open the windows every day for fresh air, bees and wasps would come in through the wide screens on the windows. The screens were designed to keep out intruders and birds, not bees and wasps. The children and their teacher would chase them out by swinging jackets, shirts, or books.

In April, they began to plan for the end-of-school picnic. Everyone in the community was invited for the Friday after-noon festivities on the weekend before school ended. This would be the final activity at the school until classes began the following September. The custom was for every family to bring part of a meal to share with other families. Miss Helen's sister Laurena and one of her friends joined the other members of the Hussman family for the picnic at Orion. That afternoon, the men and boys played baseball and pitched horseshoes. The women and girls fixed the food, caught up on the gossip, and enjoyed the last community outing that most of them would have until the end of the summer. The little children played along the edge of the canyon. Some of the little girls played school. Each family had brought lots of food, so the eating continued until late afternoon. Stella and John were proud that their daughter had finished her first year of teaching and had been rehired for the next year.

The next few days were very busy for Helen. She had to prepare the school to be closed over the summer and had to have all of her records in the mail to the county superintendent before she left on Friday afternoon. These forms consisted of census, annual, and cumulative records. The census record for each pupil was needed to determine the public-school load in local school districts as well as in the state. The pupil's annual record showed detailed scholarship and attendance for each year of the pupil's school life. This record also contained some information for guidance purposes in schools not having a regular guidance program. The pupil's cumulative record was the summary of attendance, scholarship, and extracurricular activities during the pupil's career in public common schools. If a pupil moved, the records would be forwarded from the county superintendent's office to the correct school. Each county superintendent was responsible for summarizing all of the information from each of his teachers in his district report to the state superintendent for part of the latter's annual report to the state legislature.[33]

Each school board had the responsibility of completing records to submit to the county superintendent. These included the minutes of all school board meetings, the financial reports, and any other information pertinent to the school.[34] The officers of each school district consisted of a director, a clerk, and a member. Each was elected by the voters in the district for a three-year term on a staggered basis. Therefore, each year a new officer was elected. The only qualifications to serve as a school-board member in Oklahoma at that time were that "he can read and write the English language, and shall be a legally qualified voter of said district."[35]

Helen stayed up late each night during the last week of school to fill out her records. She was also ending the year with her students. Late on Friday afternoon she was ready to leave Orion and Mrs. Cossell's for the summer. John picked up Helen and her belongings. She left none of her things in the schoolhouse because of the regular vandalizing of rural schools.

As they drove away from Orion, Helen's mind was on her going to Alva to begin college. She planned to attend three sessions—spring, summer, and August—so that she would qualify to get her teacher's certificate renewed without having to take another examination. She had saved her money so that she could pay her tuition and her room and board.

Helen drove to Alva with her friend Twila Donnelly. They lived in a widow's house near campus. It was handy for them to make the short walk up the hill to the daily classes. Six girls lived in the house that summer, two to a bedroom, with kitchen privileges. They had to stagger their cooking times at first, but as they began to know one another better, they often cooked and ate together. Most of the girls in the house were from around Seiling, which made it convenient to travel the sixty-five miles together back and forth on weekends. Helen was still expected to come home and help on the farm on weekends.

That summer, Helen was one of 924 students enrolled at Alva,[36] and she was very excited to be starting college. She was anxious to learn more about teaching and some new ways to work with her pupils at Orion. She was once again disappointed that the professors did not acknowledge that most of their students in the spring, summer, and August sessions were actually experienced teachers in rural schools. They were treated like average college freshmen who had just completed high school.

Helen and her friends often discussed the fact that their courses addressed techniques for teaching twenty-five to thirty children in one grade and never talked about how to deal with all eight grades at once. A one-room-school teacher couldn't give twenty to thirty minutes to one subject. It was difficult for Helen and her friends to study the information given to them because it seemed so irrelevant.

However, it was not all work. During one evening in the first week of spring term, Helen, Twila, her cousin Bertha, and some other girls attended a carnival held on the outskirts of Alva. As they walked around the carnival grounds together, they saw a group of boys talking. Bertha urged the other girls to go over and say hello. She had seen Lon Morris in the group and was still trying to get a date with him. The girls formed a circle around the group of boys and they talked and laughed together. Helen felt a little unsure of herself in that situation, so she just smiled and didn't say anything. She looked at Lon, who had a black felt hat perched on one side of his head and a cigarette dangling from the corner of his mouth. She wondered how Bertha was going to manage to catch him. His dark eyes flashed as he looked around the circle of girls without actually looking at any one of them in particular. Soon Lon told the other guys that he had to be moving on. The group broke up and Helen's group moved on around the carnival, with Bertha swooning over Lon at every turn. Bertha reluctantly agreed to go home after several hours when they did not see him again.

In mid-June, Helen met a young man named Johnny, who was from Covington. Although he was not much taller than she, Helen found him to be quite attractive. They often double- or triple-dated with the others in the house. Helen became very good friends with Olive Moore, another girl in the house. Helen and Johnny and Olive and her dates went out together often. Olive went home with Helen on several weekends. Twila had begun to go with Bennie Woodson, Lon Morris's best friend. Twila and Bertha would always talk about Lon when they were together, but Helen was too busy to care much about what they were saying.

During the hot Oklahoma summer, the temperature would often stay above 100 degrees for several days at a time. It would sometimes get as hot as 110 degrees. The walk up the dusty road to the classrooms wasn't too pleasant for the students when it was already scorching hot as they left the house at 8:00 A.M. After they sat through a three-hour class in a hot classroom and walked back to the boardinghouse in the stifling heat, it was not easy for the girls to study. However, because many of them were in the same classes, the task was made more enjoyable by studying together.

In the August term Helen took a course titled Tests and Measurements from Professor Morris, who was no relation to Lon. From the first class, Helen felt that the professor was putting her and her friends down because they were so inexperienced and were from the country. All of the girls studied very hard for his class. One evening they worked particularly hard on a project which called for them to apply some concepts to groups of children numbering in the hundreds. As they carried out the preliminary activity of flipping a coin five hundred times and recording the number of heads and the number of tails, none of the girls could understand how it would help them in their schools.

The next day, after Professor Morris had gone over the theory behind what they had done, Helen raised her hand. When he called on her, Helen stood up and asked him how in the world she could apply that to her schoolroom of sixteen children in all eight grades. Helen saw his face begin to turn red. He started to shake his finger in her face and began to sputter, "Miss Hussman, how dare you ask such a question!" She did not hear what he had said after that. There was a roar in her ears and her knees began to shake. She felt like running out of the room and never returning to college. Helen sat down but was numb the rest of the class period.

When the class ended, the other students surrounded Helen. They said they were so glad she had asked the question that none of them had the courage to ask. They told her not to pay any attention to what the professor had said to her. Helen felt relieved. She was glad she had not given in to her urge to cry; however, she resolved never again to tangle with Professor Morris. Helen was glad that none of her other professors acted that way toward their students.

August term ended and Helen passed all of her courses. She said good-bye to her new friends at Alva, promising to see them at the teachers' meeting in October. Helen also said good-bye to Johnny, reminding him that she would be back in October. She had lots of things to do to prepare for the opening of school in September.

T W O

HARD TIMES COME TO ORION

Helen returned from her summer in college to her farm home at Seiling to get ready to go back to Orion School for her second year of teaching. She had only two weeks between the August session and the first day of classes, and there was much to do. Helen wanted some new dresses and needed to be present for the fittings as her mother made them. Since she had been away most of the summer, for the first time, she had a lot of family and neighborhood news to catch up on. She would again be staying with the Cossells. Helen realized that she had missed them over the summer, although she hadn't thought too much about them. She was especially eager to see her pupils.

At the first teachers' meeting at Fairview, held on the first of September, Helen learned that the new board member of Orion School was a woman with three little children. The woman's oldest daughter would be a beginner at Orion. Helen met the new teacher at the school at Phroso, the next school north of Orion; her name was Vivian Becker and she was a first-year teacher. Helen liked her immediately and they planned to work together, because Mrs. Cossell's house was close to Phroso School. Helen heard everyone talking about how hard the times were getting. It was 1930, and the economy of the entire country was not doing well. However, Helen was looking forward to her first paycheck. She had spent most of her savings at college.

The teachers got together before going home from Fairview and talked about all of the requirements they were expected to fulfill in their jobs. They all wondered whether the new materials would really help them. They agreed to get together at the fall teachers' meeting at Alva to compare notes.

When Helen got to the schoolhouse on the first day of school, she was greeted by the sight of a new merry-go-round in front of it. It was a huge one, about ten feet across and six feet tall at the center. The big metal pipe that formed its axis was set in concrete, and the seats were made of boards two inches thick. It looked like it had been made to last a long time. The new merry-go-round made the rest of the schoolyard look even more desolate, but Helen was delighted that her community had decided to buy something for the children's play. Many happy hours would be spent by children whirling on that piece of equipment.[1]

The first days of school were filled with excitement. Helen had fourteen children and only six grades to teach. All of the pupils seemed to be glad to be back in school. The school board did not allow Louis back in school because he was now considered too old. The enumeration which took place over the summer indicated that no new families had moved into the district since the previous year, so there were no new pupils to replace those who had completed the eighth grade or those who had moved away with their families. Helen knew this was not good news for her, because the money which paid her salary and supported the school came from taxes paid and from state funds allocated according to the number of children in the district. As the days passed, Helen began to see indications that the Orion community was suffering from the economic depression she had been hearing about.

Helen noticed that Mrs. Cossell was fixing meatless suppers of bread and gravy more often. She hadn't been aware of how much the twenty dollars per month she paid for room and board had been needed until Mrs. Cossell asked her to pay in advance this year. After being away in Alva for the summer, Helen noticed more the poverty in which the Cossells and other families at Orion lived.

Helen saw her new friend Vivian often. She showed Vivian the notebooks she had made the year before and described how she had organized her lessons. They worked together incorporating the material from the newly approved textbooks. They knew the children would be responsible for the new material on the county examinations, and each agreed to invite the patrons from the other's school to school programs, since there was no point in competing when so little money was available. They planned a box supper for the end of September, to be held at Orion, and advertised it through the Phroso schoolchildren. They put up notices at Orion, Bado, Phroso, and Chester. The Orion pupils were excited and began enthusiastically to prepare for the program. They hoped their mother would have their new school dresses finished by the night of the program. During the summer, they had ordered new shoes and the material for their dresses out of the catalog.

The evening of the box supper arrived, with a large and generous crowd of more than fifty people in attendance. This was surprising, given the economic situation. Helen was elated that she made more money than she had the year before. The Hedrick girls sang as beautifully as ever, and Helen noticed that they were wearing new shoes and new dresses. In most families at the new school, all of the children wore shoes that looked basically alike. However, the Hedrick girls had each chosen a different style of shoe to wear. Helen knew their parents did not have much, because their father hired out as a farmhand and the girls helped their mother cook for harvest crews. She admired the Hedricks' pride in their children.

As Helen and Vivian had agreed, the next school program, in October, would be held at Phroso. Vivian asked if the Hedrick girls could come and sing there. The girls were flattered to be asked and Helen said she would borrow her father's car and take them. She also offered to help Vivian plan a Halloween party and pie supper to raise money for Phroso School.

Because she didn't have to plan a program for October, Helen began to think more and more about the upcoming teachers' meeting at Alva. She wrote a note to Johnny reminding him of when she would be there and carefully chose her dresses for the trip. When the time arrived, she met Twila at Chester and they drove to Alva together. There was a speaker from the new state curriculum committee who told them about current school-improvement efforts. In the afternoon session, they looked at the Model School Score Card and the Instructional Score Card. Helen could not imagine having anyone come to her little school to use the score cards. Once again it seemed to her that the speakers were not talking about anything that related directly to her or to her kind of school. The afternoon seemed to drag.

As soon as the meeting was over, Helen and Twila went over to Bertha's house to change. They had arranged to meet their dates at Nall's Café. Twila's date, Bennie, was right on time. He sat down with Helen and Twila to wait for Johnny. They waited and they waited. Johnny did not come. Bennie asked some of the college guys who were sitting at another table if they knew where Johnny might be. One of them said Johnny had gone home to Covington for the weekend.

Helen could not believe it. Why hadn't he told her? He knew she was coming this weekend. Now here she was, all dressed up and no place to go. She was mortified that he had made a fool of her. She wanted to cry, but she would never let anyone see her cry.

Twila felt terrible for Helen. She told her that she and Bennie would take her back to Bertha's house. Helen walked stiffly to the car and got in the front seat with Bennie and Twila. Her face burned with shame and anger with Johnny. She could hardly wait for them to get to Bertha's house so that she could go inside and be by herself.

All of a sudden Helen felt the car swerve into the curb. Bennie said, "There's a date for you, Helen. It's old Lon Morris. We'll get him for you." Before Helen could say any-thing, Bennie jumped out of the car and ran over to his friend. Lon was sitting on the fender of a car, holding his head. Bennie grabbed him by the arm and pulled him over to the car. Helen looked back down at her hands in her lap as they got to the car door. Bennie told Lon to get in. Helen leaned up as he opened the car door and crawled into the back seat. Lon asked Helen if she were going to get in the back seat with him. "No" she replied curtly as her green eyes snapped and she slammed the door shut.

Off they buzzed three in the front seat and one in the back. Helen couldn't believe it. First she had been stood up by Johnny, and now she was saddled with that cocky Lon Morris. She was miserable.

Bennie asked Lon what in the world had happened to his head. Helen had noticed that his face was fiery red. Lon explained that he had been shaving and in the mirror had seen something move behind him. Before he knew what had happened, his roommate, Pat McGhee, had poured a pokey on his head. A pokey was made to use on cattle, so it was very strong. The stuff had run all the way down Lon's face before he could get it off. Bennie began to laugh. "It serves you right, Lon. You are always playing tricks on everyone else. I'm glad old Pat finally got you one."

Twila directed Bennie to the city park, where he stopped the car near one of the picnic tables. They got out of the car and walked over to the table. It was a nice evening and the park was still green even after the hot summer. Helen looked at Lon. He really looked pitiful. The hair on the top of his head was pretty thin and she could see the fiery red color of the skin. When he looked at her, she could see that his eyes were awfully red, too. She couldn't help but lose some of the edge off her pain as she looked at him.

Soon they were all talking and laughing together. They decided to go and get something to eat. When they got back into the car, Helen got into the back seat with Lon. The rest of the evening went very fast. Helen learned that Lon was from Kansas and that his real name was C. A. Bennie said they called him Lon because he could make his face look like Lon Chaney, the movie star who acted in horror films. Helen liked the name C. A. better than Lon, so that is what she started calling him. Later he told her that his full name was Clarence Aubrey but that he hated it. Only his mother insisted on calling him Clarence.

Bennie and C. A. dropped the girls off at Bertha's before midnight. When they got to their bedroom, Helen could hardly believe the turn of events. She was still furious with Johnny for standing her up and she was surprised that she had found C. A. to be such a nice person. He liked to talk a lot and kept everyone laughing, but he wasn't at all cocky, as she had thought.

The next morning right after breakfast, the telephone

rang. C. A. was calling Helen to ask her to go out for lunch before she had to go back to Seiling. Although it was a little awkward with Bertha feeling the way she did about him, Helen said she would very much like to go. Just as she was getting ready, the telephone rang again. It was Johnny. He had come back to Alva early so that he could see her before she had to go home. He explained to Helen that he had gone home on business and not been able to avoid the trip. Helen told him that she was sorry she had missed him but that she had other plans for the morning. She never went out with Johnny again.

C. A. didn't have a car, so he walked Helen to the drugstore for lunch. His face and eyes had lost most of their redness by that time. He talked to Helen about the football team and was proud of its winning season. C. A. had a football scholarship and worked around the campus for his room and board. One of the jobs he talked about was mowing the football field. Helen was fascinated as she listened to him describe the mowing races with hand mowers on Newby Field. She knew a great deal about mowing hay with teams of horses but had never seen or heard about mowing a football field by hand. C. A. bragged that he always won the mowing races and that it helped him stay in shape to push the lawnmower. Helen enjoyed hearing him talk about his experiences on campus. As C. A. walked Helen back to the house, he told her to let him know when she was coming back because he would like to see her again. Helen explained that she probably wouldn't be back until spring term in May but that she would be sure to let him know when she was coming.

On the way back to Chester, Twila and Helen chattered about their weekend. Twila said everyone had been impressed when C. A. had called her so soon. She told Helen that everyone said C. A. had traveled all over the country and had left a girl in every city. Helen smiled as she remembered that very kind look in those big brown eyes.

Back at Orion, Helen and her pupils helped Vivian complete the plans for her Halloween party and fund-raiser. At first, Helen's community had been disappointed that the party was not going to be at Orion. However, after they were reminded of the success of the September box supper at their school and the number of people who had come from the other community, they agreed that the communities should help each other. They put up their signs in several local stores and post offices. Many young couples went to fund-raisers and school programs on their dates. There were few other places a young man could take his girl in the small communities of western Oklahoma.

Helen noticed that the children were bringing less and less for lunch. Leota Hedrick told Miss Helen that she had spent the night with one of the other girls and that when they went to the kitchen to fix their lunches for school, all they had was bread. There was nothing to put inside to make a sandwich.

Although Helen was helping with the party, she asked Millard Cossell to go as her escort. She asked him to meet her there because she was transporting the Hedrick girls to sing; however, he insisted that he drive them all over to Phroso that evening to the Halloween party. Helen took two pies Donna had baked for her. There was another good turnout, and Vivian raised as much as Helen had raised at the September program. Helen enjoyed being with Millard, and they went to several parties together that fall and winter.

One morning in November, Helen awoke to find snow on her bed. When there was a lot of wind and heavy snow, it sifted in through the cracks in the old house. As Helen left the house that morning, she noticed that a couple of

Mrs. Cossell's chickens were lying dead on the back door-step. She figured they had been looking for food and had frozen to death. Mrs. Cossell fixed fried chicken that evening and for several evenings after that. Helen couldn't help but wonder if they were just eating the chickens as they starved to death.

The snow stayed on the ground for over a week. During this time Helen had to walk the long way to school along the road. At recess she and the children went out in the snow and played fox-and-geese. They always had a lot of fun, but were glad to get back inside to the warmth of the stove.

After a couple of days of snow cover, Helen noticed that one little girl and her younger brother always went to the outhouse just as the others got out their lunches at noon. Helen asked the little girl what they were eating for lunch. The little girl told her that they had been eating snow lettuce. Helen knew that this meant they were eating the green grass under the snow. She gave her lunch to the children. She realized that she could not give her lunch to the children every day because she, too, needed to eat. She had noticed that the other children were bringing less and less to eat, and decided on a plan to help them all.

That afternoon, she suggested to the children that with their parents' permission they could cook their lunch on the woodstove. She explained that if each one of them would bring something, such as a potato or carrot, they could make soup that they could all share. The children liked the idea very much and discussed what they would need. Each of them would need a bowl or cup and a spoon, and they also would need a sharp knife and a big pot with a lid. Everyone agreed on what they could bring from home. The next day, the children arrived with the utensils they had agreed to bring, plus potatoes, carrots, onions, and dried beans. For the rest of the winter, Miss Helen would put a pot of water on the stove every morning and they would add whatever they had available. The older girls washed the dishes and cleaned up after lunch.

Cleatus, one of the little boys, could run very fast and bragged that he could catch a rabbit. One afternoon Helen decided to let him try. In less than a half-hour, he came back carrying a squirming rabbit in his hand. Helen killed and dressed the rabbit and hung it in the schoolroom for the night. They had rabbit stew the next day. Helen often let Cleatus go rabbit hunting in the afternoon so that they could have some meat in their soup.

Helen noticed that the two little children who had been eating snow lettuce were coming to school looking very hungry. One morning she asked the little girl what she had eaten for breakfast. The little girl began to cry and told her that her daddy had left three days before on an old horse with only a halter around its neck and no saddle and that they had run out of food. That afternoon Miss Helen sent a bag of dried beans home with the little girl.

The next morning, the little girl happily told Miss Helen they had eaten beans for supper and beans for breakfast and there were enough left that they would have beans again for supper that night. Helen heard that the father returned a day or two later with bags of food. Some of the people in the community said they believed he had stolen them. The neighbors were glad he had found food for his family, regardless of how he got it. The family soon moved away. Helen was glad she could spend weekends at her home where there was still plenty to eat.

One weekend, Stella suggested to Helen that she bring the Hedrick girls home with her and arrange for them to sing at a school program near Seiling. The girls were very excited about the prospect of a weekend away from home, especially with Miss Helen. When they arrived at the Hussman farm, they marveled at the farmhouse in which Miss Helen's family lived. The only houses around Orion were two- or three-room wooden structures which were small and shabby in comparison to the two-story stone house. Stella and Donna fixed a lot of food for the guest performers. The Hussmans had an abundance of canned and cured meat, canned vegetables, and many breads and sweets. The girls did themselves proud with their performance and everyone had a very good time that weekend. The next week, the girls could hardly wait to tell everyone about the fancy house that Miss Helen lived in and the feast her mother had prepared for them.

The Orion program to celebrate Thanksgiving was poorly attended. Times were getting harder, there was a lot of sickness, and the weather was bitterly cold. Helen and Vivian had advertised and had asked parents to bring cakes or cookies. They furnished the hot chocolate and coffee. The children had prepared their program, although many of them had been absent because of sickness. Only the parents of the children attended that night.

Helen and Vivian decided to plan separate Christmas parties for each community and a ciphering match for the pupils of the two schools on the Friday before. Although the times were getting harder all the time, the children were very excited about the coming of Christmas. Early in December, the Orion pupils began to plan for decorations for their tree and for the party. They also began to practice in earnest for the ciphering match against Phroso. Helen borrowed a car from her father to take the children the four and a half miles to Phroso to the match. She also got one of the parents to take a carload of children. Children from each school won some of the matches. The results were so close that they decided to call it a draw. All of the children enjoyed themselves. Later in the year they had other matches between the schools in geography, spelling, and volleyball, as well as ciphering. They also took turns giving performances in front of the children from the two schools.[2]

Helen bought each of her pupils a pencil in addition to the usual bag of fruits, candy, and nuts that Christmas. For many of the children, these would be all the goodies they would receive for Christmas in 1930. All fifty members of the community came to the school Christmas party. Helen was touched by how happy everyone seemed, even though she knew how worried many of them were about money. They sang around the Christmas tree, drank coffee and hot chocolate, and shared cakes, cookies, and other goodies. At the end of the party, they shouted "Merry Christmas!" as they hugged and shook hands with their neighbors.

Helen's whole family was together that Christmas. She enjoyed the holidays and the excitement of having friends and family around. They had had many good times as a family, but they also had had many heated discussions or arguments. All of the Hussman children had strong personalities, and they often had disagreements. The fiery tempers would result in sharp words, which would just add fuel to the fire. Sometimes Helen thought her brother took the opposite side of any issue just to create an argument. Donna, although she was much younger than the others, could hold her own in any discussion or argument. She had learned early that she must not give way to tears. Although she was only fourteen years old, Donna had started going with a young man from Chester named Art Louthan. They were often teased by Ernie and the other family members. Donna had lots of practice in sticking up for herself.

Although she had enjoyed the holidays and her twenty-first birthday, it was almost a relief for Helen to turn her thoughts back to her schoolroom. She had to begin preparing her pupils for the county examinations and also assist Vivian as she got her pupils ready, too. They worked together many evenings. Helen thought it was interesting how much she had depended on Mable the previous year, this year, Vivian was just as dependent on Helen.

Helen continued to fix soup or rabbit stew for lunch. Actually, she found that Mrs. Cossell was not able to make very much for her to eat. For supper they often had white gravy—made with just lard, flour, and water—and bread. They rarely had meat anymore. Helen was glad that Mrs. Cossell still made excellent bread.

One morning in early January, they heard a car pull up to the schoolhouse. The children looked out and announced that it was the county superintendent, who had arrived for his annual visit. Helen continued with the recitations; however, she wondered what Mr. Weaver would think of the pot of soup that was just beginning to boil on the stove. She looked back at the bowls, cups, and spoons which were lined up on the old organ with the lunch buckets of the few children who still brought some food for lunch. "Oh well," she thought, "I'm doing the very best that I know how." She had heard a few teachers talk about doing some cooking in their schoolrooms, so her thoughts returned to the subjects she was teaching to the children.

As he had done the year before, Mr. Weaver watched what was going on, talked briefly with a couple of the children, and looked around the room. He did not seem to pay any mind to the pot that was boiling on the stove. During recess, the children played a game of steal-the-bacon in the schoolroom. There was a lot of laughter as different children tried to take the blackboard eraser out from under the desk of the child who was "it" without being detected. It was a good inside game which would keep the children relatively calm. They did take a few minutes to run outside to the outhouses and to play a little in the snow before returning to their lessons. Shortly after Helen had the children back at their studies, Mr. Weaver walked out of the door. They heard his car start up and leave down the road. It was as though he had never been there at all.

One evening in February, Mrs. Cossell sat down with Helen and told her some bad news. They were going to have to sell out because they could not make it financially anymore. She told Helen that the other woman on the school board had agreed that Helen could board with her. Helen was stunned. She had never dreamed things were that bad. She took a look at Mrs. Cossell's sad face and realized that she was being very selfish to think of her concern about herself when the Cossells were losing everything. She would have to adjust to a new living arrangement only temporarily, but for the Cossell family, the hard economic times had created a situation that would drastically change their lives.

Helen and the children had a Valentine's Day party. The room was decorated with red and white, and several mothers managed to get the ingredients to bake some cookies. The children enjoyed performing for their parents, but there was a sadness among the adults that affected the children.

On the following Saturday, there was a sale at the Cossell farm. They sold all of the livestock that were left and all of the farm machinery. The two younger boys stayed in the house and tried to make a living there. Mrs. Cossell went to live with her daughter. Helen did not know what happened to Millard, because he left without saying goodbye. Helen had packed all of her belongings when John picked her up on Friday. The quilt top and pillow with the log cabin and pine trees would always remind her of the evenings she spent with Mrs. Cossell and her sons.

Helen's new living arrangement was not very good. The

family had a two-room house and had three little children. The only place for Helen to sleep was on an army cot she had brought from her home and put behind the cookstove. She had no privacy. She had to wait until the family went to bed before she could get ready for bed. At least at Mrs. Cossell's, Helen had been able to hang a curtain around her bed, giving her a little private space. But worst of all, the woman's husband was a drunkard. Sometimes he would arrive home very late and very drunk. There was no heat in the couple's bedroom, and Helen would hear the wife begging him to get into bed so he wouldn't freeze to death. Helen had not been around a problem drinker before. She had seen her dad and brother and other members of her family drink some now and then. They had wine and canyon run (their name for homemade whiskey) around the house. Actually she had tried it a couple of times herself, but she had never been around a drunk before.

Helen turned all of her energies toward school. She continued to work with Vivian, even though they now lived farther apart. They carried out their matches between the schools. Helen borrowed John's car often so she could take the children to Phroso to the matches, and also so she could go home directly from school on Fridays. She never begged her dad to stay at Orion anymore. The parties and dances at the Holubs' were not worth being behind the stove, listening to the pain the family suffered.

In March, the lady with whom she was living told Helen that the school board had met and wanted her to stay another year. Helen was relieved that she had been asked to stay; however, she was not at all happy with where she was living. She knew that jobs were not easy to come by, and she felt fortunate that she had a job. As Helen accepted the contract for the next year, she knew that she would have to find someplace else to live.

That spring, Helen and Vivian decided to have a combined program for the patrons of both communities so that the children could show off some of the things they had learned. The Hedrick sisters had learned several new songs and had taught some of the other children the words. Between the two schools, there were a number of children who could perform well. Since Helen had the last combined effort at Orion in November, they planned to have this one at Phroso. The community members needed something uplifting after such a cold, hard winter. The schoolroom was filled on the evening of the program. The adults joined in on many of the songs, and for a few minutes they seemed able to forget their worries.

In March, it was time to prepare the pupils for the county examinations. This year Helen had only two pupils who would take the examinations: Lula Hedrick had to take the eighth-grade tests, and her sister Helen had to take the seventh-grade ones. They could study together for composition, domestic science, geography, Oklahoma history, and U.S. history. In addition, Lula had to study for arithmetic, civics and grammar. Helen Hedrick also had to study for physiology and hygiene, spelling, and writing. Each year the requirements by the state were changed somewhat. Helen and Vivian had carefully gone over the new materials from Mr. Weaver to make sure they were preparing their pupils properly. They were both acutely aware that a teacher's reputation and career rode on the success of her pupils.

As she had done the year before, Helen held Saturday sessions to drill the girls in the subject areas. She went back to her family's farm on Saturday evening after the sessions. Vivian and Helen tried holding a combined session one Saturday, but it got too confusing because the children didn't know one another well enough to study together and began to socialize rather than study.

The examinations were held at Fairview on April 17, 1931. Miss Helen took Lula and Helen in her car, and they stayed all night with one of Miss Helen's friends. The main talk among the teachers was about the election of a new county superintendent, George W. Spenner. They all wondered what kinds of changes this would mean for them. Another major topic was the upcoming spring term at college. Everyone complained about the amount of record-keeping they were expected to do, and they wondered what in the world the county superintendent did with all of those records anyway. They also discussed the economic hard times. Several teachers had not been able to cash their warrants without paying the bank a penalty. Helen guessed she wasn't too bad off after all.

Lula soon received the results of her examinations and was thrilled to report to Miss Helen that she had passed. Her highest score was 96 percent in arithmetic and her lowest score was 60 percent in spelling. Helen Hedrick had also passed all of her seventh grade examinations. Miss Helen was as excited as the girls. She felt that because she had taught them for two years she had really been their teacher and that their success reflected on her competency as a teacher.

Helen and the children planned for the end-of-the-year picnic. Again the community wanted to come for a Friday picnic. John and Stella Hussman came in their new car, bringing Donna and one of her girlfriends along for the fun. John also had a new camera. In the middle of the afternoon, he got everyone together for a group picture beside the schoolhouse. Helen posed with some of her pupils next to her dad's car and also on the new merry-go-round. The eating and playing lasted until late in the afternoon.

There was also some business to be conducted by the school board. There was a vacancy on the board since Mrs.

Orion School community members pose for the photographer, John Hussman, at the end-of-the-year picnic held in May 1931.

Miss Helen with nine of her fourteen students in front of John Hussman's car.

Orion School community children on their new merry-go-round.

Miss Helen with three of the Orion community boys on the school merry-go-round.

Cossell had moved away. The picnic qualified as a public meeting for the purpose of doing school-board business. An election for the new board member was held, and Jim Holub was elected without opposition. His parents, who had held the community dances in their home, had moved, and Jim was getting married soon. He and his brother would continue to live in their parents' house a mile and a half east of the school. Helen thought it would be nice to have a young person on the school board. They had Jim take the oath,[3] and then they continued with the picnic.

Helen worked late each night of the last week of school. Although she had fewer pupils than the year before, it still took her a long time to get all of the records completed. On Friday afternoon she had everything ready to go into the mail to the county superintendent's office. She had her belongings in the back of her car so she could move them to the farm for the summer. She hurried so she would be ready to go to Alva on Sunday afternoon. She wondered whether C. A. would be there and whether he would remember who she was. After her lesson with Johnny, she didn't want to get her hopes up and then be disappointed. Helen had not told her folks much about C. A.; actually, she didn't know too much about him herself. Helen met Vivian and they went to Alva together. They had arranged to be roommates for the term in one of the boardinghouses near campus.

ROMANCE LEADS TO MARRIAGE

Vivian and Helen chattered all the way to Alva, wondering who would be there for spring term and hoping their courses would be interesting. Helen told her about her tangle with Professor Morris. They both needed to complete the courses to qualify for the next-level teaching certificate. Helen could get her second-grade certificate if she attended all three terms. Her hopes of learning things that would help her in her schoolroom were getting dimmer. None of the teachers' meetings or workshops during her first two years of teaching nor the courses she had taken so far had helped her.

As the girls began arriving at the rooming house, the catching up on gossip began in earnest. Helen heard that Bertha Donnelly had finally gotten her chance at Lon Morris. They had double-dated with Bennie and Twila a few times; however, everyone said nothing had come of it. In fact, everyone was still talking about the way Lon had just disappeared from school right after football season. No one knew where he had gone. He had not dropped his classes, so he got F's in everything for the semester. He had just reappeared one day and seemed to be okay. He sure was a mysterious fella, they decided.

Classes began on Monday morning and Helen made

the now-familiar walk up the hill to the classrooms. She couldn't help but wonder what had caused C. A. to leave and return so abruptly. Her class began well, and she discovered that she knew most of the people who were enrolled. That evening, she and Vivian and several others from the rooming house went to Nall's Café. Helen looked around at the tables expectantly, hoping that C. A. would be there. However, he was not. Helen's attention turned back to her companions and their discussion of what had happened in their classes that day. Soon Helen saw C. A. come bouncing through the door, talking and laughing with the guy that was with him. As soon as he saw Helen, he came right over to her table. Pulling up a chair from another table, he sat down and began talking to her about nothing in particular. The sparkle in his eye indicated that he was glad to see her. After he asked the girls where they were staying, he got up and left as abruptly as he had sat down. He went over to a table of boys and sat down with them. Helen wasn't sure what all of that meant, but she recognized that she was certainly glad to see him.

When they finished eating, Helen and her friends got up to leave. C. A. had not looked her way again. The girls took the long way to the door so that they would pass by the table where C. A. and the other boys sat. All of the boys said "Good-bye" and "We'll be seeing you" as the girls left. Helen caught C. A.'s eye as she walked by, but he did not say anything special to her.

The girls talked excitedly as they walked toward their rooming house. Each of them had picked out someone in the café that they would like to get to know and they were all excited that Helen seemed to have someone already.

"He came right over as soon as he saw you."

"He found out where you were staying."

In spite of their enthusiasm, Helen's heart was heavy.

She could visualize the way C. A. had bounded into the café with the cigarette hanging out of the corner of his mouth. She chuckled to herself as she remembered that a year ago she had thought that he was cocky. "Well," she thought, "at least he remembered who I am and came over to talk."

Within days C. A. called and asked Helen to go out for supper with him. Everyone in the house was excited for her. Vivian waved her hair three times before Helen was satisfied with the way it looked. She put on her prettiest dress and waited for C. A. to arrive. His knock was heard at the exact time he had said he would pick her up. He still did not have a car, so they walked to a little café in town.

That evening, C. A. explained that he had very little money and that he was working a day job and a night job to try to get enough money to pay his tuition. He told Helen he suffered from terrible headaches and had heard about the Mayo Clinic in Rochester, Minnesota. During the fall his headaches had become so unbearable that he just left school and went up to see if the Mayo Clinic could help him get some relief. C. A. explained that although he had hitchhiked most of the way, the cost of room and board and the surgery on his sinuses, plus the costs that he had to pay for his room at Alva, had wiped out his small savings. By leaving without going through the proper paperwork, he had lost his football scholarship for the next semester. He told her that he definitely felt better but that he was sure one poor guy.

Helen was glad he had told her about what had happened. She was sorry he had suffered so much, but was relieved that it wasn't a worse story. Her imagination had run wild when she heard about his leaving so suddenly.

Helen and C. A. began to spend a lot of time together. Soon everyone started referring to them as a couple. However, Helen still enjoyed the company of other girls in the rooming house. Her friend from the summer before, Olive Moore, arrived in time for the summer session. They always had a good time together.

Helen's parents still expected her at the farm on weekends. She began to tell her family about her new fella. By now, C. A. had told her a lot about himself. He had described his travels and adventures all across the country. In 1925, when he was seventeen years old and a junior in high school, he and his best friend, Pete Miller, were working in a bakery in Iola, Kansas, wrapping bread. They put their money together and bought a 1923 Ford Classic automobile. They built a bed in the back and decided to take it to California that summer. In the first part of June, still owing twenty-five dollars on the car and with three dollars between them, they headed west. They worked in the wheatfields at Pratt, Kansas, and made sixty-six dollars. After sending twenty-five dollars back home to pay off the car and putting another twenty-five dollars in the bank in Pratt, they took the remaining money and went to Colorado. They began to have car trouble and had to put a boot on one of the tires. They could not find work anywhere. They tried Trinidad, Colorado, and Santa Fe, and Albuquerque, New Mexico; still no work. The Kansans camped near the San Jose River and sent for their money from Pratt. When the money arrived, they got some new tires for the car and went on to Arizona. The engine in their car began acting up and they had to be towed into the next town. It took the last of their money to get the car back on the road again. C. A. and Pete picked up a hitchhiker outside Kingman, Arizona. The hitchhiker told the boys about riding the rails on to California, where the hobo camps were located, and how to get on trains without getting caught. Pete and C. A. decided to leave their ailing car in Kingman and follow the hitchhiker's advice about the trains.

They made it fine to Needles, California, and on to Barstow. However, at Barstow, coffee was twenty cents a cup; they couldn't afford to buy anything. They wound up eating with the hobos who frequented this route. They took a Union Pacific freight out of Barstow to San Bernardino. However, when the train pulled into the freight yard, they were caught by the railroad police and were put in jail for five days for vagrancy.

They decided to leave the rail riding to others and hitchhike to Los Angeles. They discovered that they could get rides faster if there were just one person, so they decided to split up and meet at the post office in Los Angeles. The first one there would leave a message for the other one at general delivery. Pete got the first ride, but soon C. A. was picked up by a candy salesman from Los Angeles. His wife's brother was also on the road that summer, and he insisted that C. A. come to his house and stay in his brother-in-law's room. It sure sounded good to C. A. When he heard about Pete, the candy salesman agreed that he could stay, too, if they didn't mind cramped quarters.

Within two days C. A. had a job and went to meet Pete at the post office. Pete was also able to find a job within a short time. Although their room was small and hot, they enjoyed the summer in Southern California. Near the end of August, Pete and C. A. told their friends good-bye and started home. They took the train, paying this time, to pick up their car in Kingman, Arizona. They paid the repair bill and started home. Near Las Vegas, New Mexico, they had a wreck. No one was hurt, but the car would hardly run at all. The boys decided to sell it and hitchhike home for school. Each completed his senior year and graduated from Iola High School in 1926.

Helen was very interested in hearing C. A.'s stories. He had done some exciting things and could tell the stories in an entertaining way. As they got to know each other better, he told her even more about himself.

C. A.'s father was a machinist and engineer. He had helped C. A. and Pete get a job in the machine shop of Iola's foundry after they graduated; however, they had just gotten a taste of traveling around the country during the previous summer, and they were anxious to see more. They went to visit C. A.'s aunt and uncle in Kansas City, Missouri. Uncle J. L. and C. A.'s father, Aubrey, had been in a business together in the early 1920's before the bottom dropped out of everything. They operated a car dealership and a machine shop and leased the second floor of their building to the U.S. Army. After the business failure, J. L. took his family back to Kansas City. Uncle J. L. helped the boys get a job in an automobile assembly plant in Columbia, Missouri; however, they were still anxious to see more of the country.

One day they heard about a need for workers in Pontiac, Michigan, just outside Detroit; both C. A. and Pete volunteered to go. They hadn't saved much money, but they thought for sure they could make it big in Detroit. They took the train from Kansas City. The jobs lasted only two weeks, and they were let go without their final paychecks. C. A. took a job as a fry cook in a café. He had never been one before but he had watched other people do it and figured he could do it, too. What a job it turned out to be! Pete had not been able to find a full-time job, so he suggested they go on east. It didn't take much to convince C. A. to quit the job; he knew he didn't want to be a fry cook for the rest of his life.

They started out hitchhiking and arrived outside Berlin, Illinois, just before dark. As they walked into town, they were met by the sheriff, who asked what they were doing in his town. They told him they were just passing through. He told them they were not welcome there and gave them the choice of renting an expensive room in the hotel or going to jail for the night. They chose jail. The next morning, after a meager but free breakfast, Pete and C. A. began walking east. They split up and got rides through Indiana and into Ohio. It was there they ran into rain, which lasted all the way through Ohio. Although they each got rides pretty quickly, the heavy rain made them miserable. They met up in Mansfield, Ohio, and decided to spend some of their money for a room to get dry and to get a good night's sleep. Until now, they had been sleeping wherever they could find a place that was free.

The next morning they got a ride together in a truck going to Wheeling, West Virginia. They thought they had made it when they reached West Virginia. How much farther could it be to the East Coast? That late summer morning in 1926, they left Wheeling on foot. They walked and they walked. Although they saw many trucks going east on Route 40, they couldn't get a ride. They walked all the way to Washington, Pennsylvania. At that point the Kansas boys joined a hobo camp for the night and felt fortunate that they got something to eat.

Pete and C. A. decided to go their separate ways again and meet in Baltimore, Maryland. C. A. went toward Cumberland and from there got a ride in a truck that was going all the way to Baltimore. Although he had traveled quite a bit by now, he was truly impressed with Baltimore; he had not seen an old port city before. He met Pete at the post office and they spent several days seeing the sights. Fortunately, rooms and food were cheap, because they had very little money.

C. A. had always enjoyed history and at his urging Pete agreed to go toward Washington, D.C., instead of north toward New York. They started the forty miles separately. C. A. got to the Washington post office the next afternoon.

He figured that Pete probably had already made it; however, there was no message. For three days C. A. went to the post office looking for Pete. He was beginning to get very worried. The fourth day, on a hunch, he asked if there were another post office in Washington. Sure enough, there was, several blocks away. When C. A. arrived, he could see Pete pacing back and forth in front of the general delivery window. They were very glad to see each other and relieved that nothing had happened to them. Each of them had spent almost all of his money. They spent a couple more days seeing the sights of the nation's capital, then decided it was time to look for work.

After asking around, they learned that there were jobs in the Shenandoah Valley in Virginia. They left for New Market, Virginia, where there were horse farms in need of workers. They went to Court Manor Farm, where the two strong-looking young men were hired immediately. Although they had imagined they would be walking race horses or driving ladies around in carts, they were assigned to dig rocks out of the pastures. It was hard physical labor, but it was nice to have a place to sleep, plenty of good food, and some money coming in. They had been told the work was seasonal and it would end when the weather turned cold.

Pete and C. A. decided to leave Virginia and head farther south on C. A.'s birthday, November 12. He was twenty years old and they had a lot yet to see. They identified target cities in which to meet as they hitchhiked separately. Their first meeting took place in Charlotte, North Carolina, and then they headed south toward Florida. C. A. had picked up the lingo of the road as they traveled around. He was outgoing and enjoyed meeting people. From the experiences he had, both good and bad, he had learned to survive quite well. Outside Columbia, South Carolina, he was picked up by three young guys in a snazzy-looking car. They told C. A. they wanted him to drive. Although he thought it was a little strange, he agreed. As he drove down the road, the guys broke out a jar of white lightning. They passed the jar around and when it got to C. A., he took a swig out of the jar. They went on down the road talking, laughing, and drinking. One of the guys told C. A. that if there were any problems, he should say the car was his. C. A.'s head was beginning to buzz a little; he didn't drink too often and certainly not on an empty stomach.

Suddenly C. A. heard a siren and a police car pulled up beside them, signaling them to stop. As he pulled the car to the side of the road, another car filled with men in civilian clothes drove up behind them. The officers surrounded the car. When they asked who owned the car, the guys in the car pointed to C. A. One officer asked him if the car were his and C. A. heard himself say, "Yes, sir." The officers ordered them out of the car. They were searched and put into the police car. As they were driven away, C. A. could see the officers and plainclothesmen searching the car. C. A. heard the officers talking about three men in a car like theirs who had been involved in a moonshining ring and that someone had been killed in a raid. C. A. was terrified.

When they got to the police station, the officers were busy getting the three others out of the car and into the station. C. A. saw his chance and took off running. He had never been so scared in his entire life. The next few days were sheer torture and he kept expecting to be picked up by the police. When he met Pete in Jacksonville, Florida, they decided the police would not come across a state line to get him; however, C. A. continued to be nervous and was always looking over his shoulder. They did some odd jobs while they were in Florida, but decided they wanted to go home to Kansas in time for Christmas.

Their route home took them from Lake City, Florida, to Atlanta, and Macon, Georgia, and Chattanooga, Tennessee. They were successful in hitchhiking until they got to Chattanooga. It was getting very cold by that time, so Pete and C. A. decided to try the freight trains again. As they huddled together to keep warm and took turns looking out for train inspectors and their fellow travelers, they became very anxious to get home again. They made it through Memphis and on home to Iola in time for Christmas in 1926.

C. A. told Helen he had stayed pretty close to home after that. He had worked at a variety of jobs but had found nothing he wanted to do for the rest of his life. Helen asked how in the world he had ever wound up in Alva, Oklahoma. C. A. said he had worked in the wheat harvests for several summers and that was how he had come to Alva. He told her that he and a friend had been in central Oklahoma working as hired hands in the harvest fields. In August they had been hitchhiking through Alva on their way to the Kansas fields when a guy stopped them and asked if they played football. The guy went on to tell them that the coach of Northwestern State Teachers College was looking for players. C. A.'s high school team had won the Kansas state championship when he was a senior, and he had been one of the main players. He decided he might rather play football and go to college than keep working in the wheat harvest. He walked up the hill to the field house, met with the coach, and got a scholarship to attend Northwestern State Teachers College.

He told Helen that the only assistance he got from his parents was help with his laundry. He would ship his dirty clothes to his mother in Kansas, also tucking in candy and treats for his little brother, Ernest James, who was fourteen years younger than he. C. A. also had an older sister, Lauretta, who had two little girls, and a younger sister, Elvene, who was in high school. He didn't talk much about his family.

Helen loved to hear C. A. tell about his adventures; however, it did make her nervous. She knew she couldn't tell her parents about his gallivanting around, because her dad was too protective. It was bad enough that C. A. was from Kansas, was four years older than she, and smoked cigarettes.

She was still taking classes, but Helen's mind became more and more occupied with thoughts of C. A. She was taking Primary Reading during August term and there was a lot of reading assigned. However, she could not keep her mind on her books when she sat down to study. She finally made the decision to take C. A. home with her for the weekend.

Helen was excited about his seeing her home and meeting her family. He had told her a little about his family, and although the Morrises now lived on an acreage, C. A. had grown up in town. In fact, Helen learned that during the early teens and twenties, C. A.'s father had been the chief engineer for the Le Hunt cement plant and later had his own business. During that time the Morrises were considered well-to-do. Helen wondered what he would think of her family's Oklahoma farm life.

As soon as they arrived at the farm, John told C. A. he wanted C. A. to go with him to get some watermelons from the field for supper. C. A. followed John on foot. They got to the edge of the watermelon field and John told him to pick out a couple of big ones. C. A. picked out two large melons and started to pick one up. He assumed that John would get the other one. When he looked up, C. A. saw that John had picked up two watermelons and had one under each arm. C. A. moved the melon under one arm and picked up the other one as John had done.

John told him to follow him to the house. C. A. knew he was in excellent physical condition because he was already working out for the football season. As he watched John, who was fifty years old, stride toward the house with the watermelons, C. A. was determined to keep up with him. But by the time they reached the house, C. A. was several feet behind, puffing, with sweat pouring down his face. He thought his arms would drop off. John dumped his watermelons into the tank to cool and headed out the barn to work. C. A. was extremely impressed as he dropped his melons into the tank and looked for a bit of shade.

Everyone seemed to get along well. Stella cooked her usual excellent meals. Donna brought her boyfriend Art over to meet Helen's beau. Helen's brother Ernie found C. A. to be a match for his quick questions and argumentative style. The biggest problem for C. A. was when and where to smoke. He would stay with the family for as long as he could stand it and then go the outhouse. Later they teased him that they could see the smoke coming out of every crack in the outhouse when he went there. The weekend passed quickly, and soon it was time for Helen and C. A. to go back to Alva.

Helen had to take her finals and get ready for the end of the term. She had lost most of her enthusiasm for studying, and it certainly showed when she received a D in Primary Reading. Helen was mortified; she had never made such a low grade in her life. But it was the end of the summer, and she had to begin thinking about telling C. A. good-bye and getting started at Orion. C. A. promised to come down to see Helen as often as he could; however, he needed to fulfill his commitment to the football team, concentrate on his studies, and work to make some money.

Helen began her third year of teaching by driving over to the preschool teachers' meeting at Fairview by herself. Vivian had left Alva at the end of the summer term and had obtained a job in the Major County superintendent's office. The new superintendent, Mr. Spinner, had enlarged his office staff with an assistant, Miss Bertha Mae Weed, and a clerk, Vivian. All of the teachers were wondering what changes would be in store for them.

At lunch Vivian asked Helen about C. A. and did not seem surprised when she was told how close they had become. Helen's eyes sparkled as she told her friend that they planned to see each other as often as possible.

Vivian brought up the subject of where Helen planned to live. She informed Helen that the family with whom Helen had lived the previous spring had moved to the southern part of the state. Helen breathed a sigh of relief; now she would have to find a new place to live for sure. Vivian went on to tell her she had heard that the alcoholic husband had been stabbed by a Mexican. She shuddered when she remembered the drunken scenes at their house.

Later that day, Helen learned that she would have only twelve pupils that year. Mr. Spinner told her that Orion school board had suggested that Helen board with Jim Holub and his new wife, Audrey. It seemed like a good idea to Helen; it certainly couldn't be any worse than last year's arrangements.

So Helen moved into the house which had been the dance hall. It had one big room, a kitchen, and a porch. They had partitioned off three corners of the big room with curtains on wires. Jim and Audrey slept in one corner, Jim's brother Emil slept in another, and Helen had the third. The rest of the room was a kind of living room. There was a table in the kitchen where Helen could do her schoolwork after supper. However, there was no outhouse. There were two paths which led from the back porch; one led into some blackjacks and the other led to a space behind the barn. Helen and Audrey used the path into the blackjacks, where they fashioned a tree limb on which they could sit to go to the bathroom. Jim and his brother went behind the barn. Helen paid them twenty dollars per month for room and board.

Helen's father's old car, which she had used the year before, was in very poor condition, so she had to leave it at the farm most of that year. Once again she was dependent upon her father to come and get her on weekends. She walked the mile and a half to school. In addition to the decrease in the number of pupils at Orion, Helen had been told at the teachers' meeting that state aid to Major County schools had decreased from $15,368 in 1930–31 to $11,250 in 1931–32.[1] She didn't like the sound of all the decreases. She sure hoped the warrants from Orion would be good.

As she started the school year, Helen missed Lula and the other children who were no longer there. She had no trouble settling her pupils into the routines. The beginners needed a lot of attention, but the children knew what was expected of them. There were new textbooks in grades 1 through 8 in reading and penmanship and in agriculture for the boys in grade 7. Helen wondered whether the parents would be able to afford the forty-seven to eighty-three cents for reading books, the seven cents for penmanship, and the eighty-five cents for agriculture. It really wouldn't make too much difference, because she had only one child who would be taking the examinations, and Helen could make sure that she got a current copy of the book from which to study. Helen Hedrick was the only pupil who would take the county examinations in the spring of 1932.

Living with the Holubs was a different experience for Helen. Jim and Audrey were newlyweds, so they had not settled into daily routines. Often Audrey would go someplace or would go out to help Jim instead of preparing supper. Frequently it would be 10:00 or 11:00 P.M. before they ate. One evening about nine o'clock, Audrey decided to fix chicken and noodles for supper. She put a chicken on to boil and started mixing the dough for noodles. As she was rolling it out, Jim said, "That's not the way my mother made noodles." Audrey looked at him, folded the dough into a ball, took it over to the slop bucket, and threw it in. She looked at Jim and said, "I'll teach you to make fun of my noodles!"

Helen's mouth dropped open as she watched. She was starving and now their supper had been thrown into the slop bucket. She knew the chicken wouldn't be done for quite a while yet. However, Audrey had canned a lot of tomatoes that summer from their garden and was able to use some milk from their cow to make tomato soup for their supper.

The next morning Helen knew that Audrey was still peeved at Jim when she was served tomato soup for breakfast. However, Audrey had made some sandwiches for Helen's lunch and had put in the usual cookie and apple. Helen began to wonder about this living arrangement, but that afternoon when she got home from school, she smelled a good supper being cooked. Audrey was over her mad spell.

Helen planned a pie supper for the end of September and Audrey was anxious to help with it. Helen missed her friend Vivian, but Audrey and Jim were lots of fun to be around. Helen had told them about C. A. and they suggested that he come and spend the weekend with them. The pie supper would be the perfect time, they thought.

Helen wrote to C. A. and asked him to come for her pie supper and to spend the weekend with the Holubs. At first, Helen's parents were not too pleased, but they agreed that the Holubs were a nice young couple, so they didn't voice any objection to the invitation.

The pupils in the school were very excited about the pie supper and about the program. Lula agreed to come back and sing with the others. Two days before the pie supper, Helen received a card from C. A. saying he couldn't come that weekend. He had a football game and also had to work. He told her he was looking forward to seeing her at the October teachers' meeting and hoped she would ask him to come to Orion again.

Helen was very disappointed, but she went ahead with the pie supper and the program. The children always lifted her spirits, and the community depended on the events at the school for entertainment. They made some money, although it was not nearly as much as they had made with the box suppers in previous years.

In October, Helen went to Alva for the teachers' meeting and spent as much time as she could with C. A. He was interested in what was happening at her school and asked her if she were going to invite him down again. Within two weeks, he made one of his many trips to visit Helen at the Holubs'. Although Jim and Audrey had finished only the eighth grade, they enjoyed this college boy from Kansas. They played cards, told stories, and ran around to any social activity that happened to be going on. They also hunted squirrels and rabbits and went coyote hunting on horseback. Helen had never enjoyed herself any more than she did with them.

On weekends when C. A. couldn't come down, Helen usually went home to the farm. She continued to help her dad with the farm work. Between her schoolwork, the farm work, and her courtship with C. A., she was very busy.

When it began to get cold, she and the children decided to make soup again. Cleatus was still able to catch rabbits whenever he wanted, so they often had rabbit stew. Sometimes someone in the community would shoot an extra squirrel and they would have squirrel stew. But their most usual meal was vegetable soup.

Thanksgiving came and went. The school activities were well attended, but the times were very hard. As usual, the children became very excited about Christmas. They enthusiastically made decorations and then went to the canyon to get the Christmas tree. They sang carols as they decorated the tree. Helen had hoped C. A. would come for some of the Christmas holidays, but he had told her he thought he should go to Kansas to visit his family. Helen wasn't very happy about it, but she knew he was probably right.

Late one cold evening when Audrey and Jim and gone to a neighborhood card party, Helen was lying in bed thinking about C. A. Jim's brother Emil had come home early from a date with his girl and was in his bed across the room. Suddenly he asked Helen if she were awake. She said she was. He said, "Helen, you know, we sure have surprised Jim. He thought he would come home some night and find you and me in the same bed." He went on to tell Helen that he had too much respect for her to do that. Helen replied with a dry mouth that she had a lot of respect for him, too. He concluded: "Nope, they're never going to find that." By this time, Helen was wide awake, but soon she heard Emil snoring softly as he slept. He always treated Helen extra special after that, and they remained good friends.

On December 22, 1931, sometime after lunch, the children heard a car pull up outside the school. They shouted that it was a man, but they did not know who he was. Helen went to the door and recognized County Superintendent Spenner. She invited him into the room and introduced him to the children. He sat down at one of the empty desks in the back as she continued with the lesson. Helen noticed that he was writing much more than Mr. Weaver had. He seemed to be watching her and the children very closely. Helen began to get a little nervous. Then Mr. Spenner began to walk around the room, examining everything carefully. Helen was glad that the stew pot was clean and that all of the bowls and cups were neatly in the cabinet. Mr. Spenner looked carefully at the water bucket and the dipper. Helen hadn't thought too much about all of them drinking out of one dipper until she saw Mr. Spenner standing there.

When Mr. Spenner got to the Christmas tree, he asked some of the children if they had put on a Christmas program. Several of the children offered to sing for him. He looked at Helen for her reaction. Since it was 3:30, Helen decided they had all done enough work for the day and it would be fun for them to show off for the superintendent. Mr. Spenner seemed to enjoy the children, and Helen was relieved to see him smile. The half-hour went quickly and Helen reminded the children that it was time to go home. They put on their coats, hats, and gloves, and those who had lunch buckets picked them up. Few books went home so close to Christmas. The children went laughing and chattering out the door.

Mr. Spenner talked to Helen about state school-improvement efforts. He asked her if any of the school-board members had talked to her about working toward a second-class school certificate. Helen explained that the community was very poor and that she didn't think it would be able to make any improvements in the school facility. Helen looked around the shabby room with its community water bucket, the old curtains on the windows, the ancient chalkboard, the unshielded stove, and the old organ which served as a storage cabinet. She told Mr. Spenner she would be interested in working on school-improvement efforts if the school board wanted to work with her.

Mr. Spenner thanked her for her hospitality and left. Helen hurried around the schoolroom, getting ready to leave. It was almost dark and she had a mile and a half to walk home. She chuckled to herself, "I wonder what he would have said about school-improvement efforts if I had let Cleatus catch a rabbit this afternoon and he could have seen me dress it and hang it in the classroom for the night." As she walked home in the freezing cold, she thought about their conversation again. "They really just don't understand what I am dealing with here," she thought.

C. A. came to see Helen again in January. Helen asked about his visit to his family at Christmas. He just shrugged and said they were all fine. He didn't like to talk much about his family. Stella invited them over for Sunday dinner before C. A. had to go back to Alva. John's old car was back in working order, so they were able to drive over for the noon-time dinner. The whole family seemed glad to see C. A., and Stella sent a box of goodies back to Alva with him. It was almost like he was a member of the family. Helen took C. A. to the crossroads at Chester, where he hitched a ride back to school with some other students.

The days and weeks passed quickly and Helen stayed very busy. She went to help her dad whenever C. A. didn't come. They tried to arrange ahead of time when he would visit, but sometimes he got a chance for an unexpected ride and would write and tell Helen he was coming.

Late one Friday evening when Helen had gone to the

farm, they heard a knock on the door. It was C. A. He had written Helen that he was coming, but when he got to the Holubs', he found the unopened letter on the clock shelf. Since his ride had gone on and the Holubs weren't home, he had started walking to the Hussman farm. No one had passed on the road to offer him a ride, and he had walked the entire sixteen miles. The Hussmans knew then that C. A. was serious about Helen.

In March, Jim Holub told Helen the school board had met and wanted her to stay another year at Orion. Helen was flattered that she was being asked to stay, but she wanted to move to a school that was closer to her folks and where it was easier to get to and from Alva. In fact, she and C. A. were talking about getting married. They hadn't made any definite wedding plans, but Helen always liked to look ahead. She informed Jim that she would not be staying at Orion. The word soon got around that Helen was leaving and there would be a new teacher next year. The children were upset, but they knew Helen had a beau and they hoped she would get married.

Miss Helen tried to have a fairly normal end of the year. She had borrowed a science textbook for Helen Hedrick, and they prepared for all the examinations she would have to take. Miss Helen wanted to finish the year successfully for her pupils and herself; she also had to find a job for the next year.

In April when Miss Helen took Helen Hedrick for the county examinations in Fairview, she asked her friend Vivian if she knew of any schools that were open next year. Vivian told her she had heard that Chester School was looking for a teacher. At her suggestion, Helen talked to Mr. Spenner about the possibility of going to Chester. He told her he would look into it for her. Helen hoped she could get that school because it would put her right between

Alva and the farm outside Seiling. This was the main route between the two places, and it would be very easy to get rides. She crossed her fingers and hoped for the best.

Helen got a chance to go to Alva to see C. A. before the end of school. Her father's car was again out of working order, so she had to depend on getting rides with others. She had already made plans to attend all three summer sessions, but this was an extra. Helen wrote to C. A. and asked him to get her a place to stay for the weekend. They thoroughly enjoyed being together, and the weekend slipped by before they knew it. On Sunday afternoon C. A. took Helen to the place she was supposed to meet her ride, but it had already gone. They found someone else who was going to Seiling the next day, but she couldn't get there in time for school. Helen called the folks at Bado Store and asked them to send a message to Jim and Audrey that she wouldn't be back in time for school on Monday. Jim happened to be in the store at the time. He told Helen not to worry, that Audrey had always wanted to be a teacher and would substitute the next day.

Everything went just fine and Helen got to school right after lunchtime on Monday. The children had enjoyed Audrey, and Audrey had enjoyed the children and doing something different from her regular routine.

That year, the end-of-the-year picnic had a special meaning. Helen had been asked to take the teaching job in Chester. Although she was sad to leave Orion and the people she had grown to know and love, she was excited about the prospect of working in a new school that would be closer to her folks and easier for C. A. to get to. The whole community came out to tell her good-bye and good luck. Chester was only eight miles away, so they promised to come to her box and pie suppers.

Helen completed her records and on Friday evening

left Orion School for what she thought was the last time. Her mind raced up to the upcoming term at college. She had promised herself to study more and get better grades this summer. The memory of that D in Primary Reading still made her wince. With her savings, Helen had bought a 1925 Model A Ford coupé for one hundred dollars, which would make it much easier for her to get around that summer.

Helen returned to the same rooming house where she had stayed the summer before. She had arranged to room with her friend Olive. By now everything was familiar to Helen. She knew what to expect in her classes, and she had gotten to know the town very well. She and C. A. spent as much time together as possible. They began to talk seriously about getting married. He was glad she had moved to Chester School. They knew she had to work, and Chester was in a much better location for them, regardless of what they decided to about getting married.

C. A. still had a year to go to get his degree. Helen considered it very important for him to finish. She knew he wasn't terribly interested in becoming a teacher, but it was something he could fall back on, especially with the lifetime teaching certificate that went with the degree.

After much discussion, Helen and C. A. decided to get married at the end of the August session in the summer of 1932. She had not yet met C. A.'s family, but she knew that she wanted to marry him. Her family was not overjoyed by the news. Although Helen was twenty-two years old, she would be the first of the Hussman children to marry. She and her roommate, Olive, left Alva two days before the August 17 wedding. They stopped to get a new dress and all of the accessories for Helen before they went to the farm to prepare for the wedding. Stella's mother and father and her brother and his wife and two little daughters from Oklahoma City came for the wedding. Everyone pitched in to make it a memorable home wedding. C. A. was to catch a ride down from Alva on the morning of the wedding. It had been a particularly hot and dry August, even for western Oklahoma, but, on the night of August 16 there was a terrible rain, a real gullywasher. Next morning, the roads were closed, and some of the bridges had been washed out. Helen was miserable; she knew that all of her plans were ruined and there would be no wedding.

As usual, John could not bear to see his daughter unhappy. He told them to get on with the wedding plans, got into his truck, and went to get C. A. John found a way to get through to Alva and spotted a sad-looking C. A. carrying a new brown suit and trying to hitch a ride. They arrived at the farm with just enough time to get cleaned up for the 6:00 P.M. ceremony. Helen later remembered that everyone at the wedding cried except C. A., the preacher, and herself.

Helen's parents sold their best milk cow and gave the twenty-five dollars to the couple as a wedding present. After the ceremony and an abundant supper, Helen and her new husband drove to Fairview and spent their wedding night at the hotel. Their honeymoon consisted of a trip to meet C. A.'s family in Iola, Kansas, before returning to school. Helen's meeting with the Morris family went very well. She liked his little sister and brother immediately. She was also taken with C. A.'s niece, who lived with her grandparents at that time. C. A.'s mother seemed not to feel well while they were there and tended to stay in her room a lot. C. A. would take her food up to her and try to make her feel better. Helen's mother had been sick a lot when she was younger, so she understood. Helen felt comfortable helping in the kitchen and enjoyed talking to C. A.'s dad. Aubrey worked away from home a lot in cement plants. This left his wife, Ada, alone to raise their two youngest children and their grandchild and to take care of the small farm. C. A. had told Helen that at one time his parents had lived much better but now were barely able to make ends meet. Helen looked around and thought they had things very nice.

During their honeymoon, Helen and C. A. found that they were very compatible in many ways. They both liked to travel, and they both enjoyed visiting family. The time they could spend together before they prepared for school went very quickly. Soon it was time for them to return to Oklahoma to begin their married life, living apart much of the time.

F O U R

HELEN MOVES
TO CHESTER SCHOOL

At the end of their honeymoon, Helen left C. A. in Alva and drove on to her school in Chester. She arranged to stay with a member of the school board, Mrs. Jellison, who lived three miles from the school. Helen's parents had kept the Jellisons' daughter while she finished one school term, so the Jellisons agreed to let Helen share a room with their daughter for free. They also had a telephone, which meant that C. A. could call Helen once in a while.

Although the old car was very fragile, C. A. took it back to Alva with him. It did allow him to come home on many weekends and take Helen to the farm in Seiling. When the weather was good, she walked to school; when it was bad, she rode horseback with one of her pupils.

The school building at Chester wasn't quite as old or primitive as the one at Orion. Instead of a potbellied stove, it had a long one which would take a whole log. There were gas lights hanging from the ceiling, one in front of the room and one in back. The whole place looked cheerier to Helen.

At the preschool teachers' meeting at Fairview, Helen received a copy of the newly revised *Course of Study for Elementary Grades.* The state superintendent, John Vaughn, had worked long and hard to get it completed. It was a year late, but there were new, detailed teaching lessons in arithmetic, reading, composition and grammar, penmanship, spelling, geography, and history and civics. *A Teacher's Hand Book on Character Education* and lesson plans for agriculture were issued in separate pamphlets. Helen was glad to see some of the suggestions in the *Course of Study,* but she could not imagine how one person could do everything in the guide. She had nineteen pupils that year, and all eight grades were represented.

At that first teachers' meeting, Mr. Spenner, the county superintendent, told the teachers he wanted all of them to concentrate more on school improvement. He acknowledged that Major County was very poor and that their county would get only $11,704 in state aid for 1932–33. Helen listened to Mr. Spenner as he described how he would divide the funds among the schools. Although she did not understand the process very well, she figured that her school board would probably get very little extra money. The superintendent reminded the teachers that sixty-five of their schools in Major County were recognized as model schools and that twenty-eight of those were now accredited. Helen had not paid much attention to the model-school program at Orion because she never thought the school board would work on a project. She couldn't help but remember her conversation with Mr. Spenner the previous December. She was paying attention as some of the projects for school improvement were discussed. Maybe the school board at Chester would be interested in helping her, she thought. She took copies of the materials that were distributed.

This was to be a very busy year for the new Mrs. Morris. She had nineteen children to teach, new curriculum guides, and several new textbooks. This meant she had to make new outlines for the subjects that would be on the county examinations. In 1932–33 there were new textbooks in U.S.

history, civics, spelling, and music. The telephone calls from C. A. helped her get through the first lonely weeks. He was not playing football that year, so he could come to Helen's fund-raisers. He liked to help her get ready for the pie and box suppers. She missed her little singers from Orion but found that the children in Chester liked to perform also. Although Helen and C. A. were well aware of the hard times all around them and the dust storms that were becoming more and more of a problem, they were very optimistic about their future. Neither of them expected many material things, so they did not feel bad about not having many possessions.

At the October teachers' meeting in Alva, Mr. Spenner asked each teacher to identify the area on which he or she was going to focus for school improvement. Helen had read the material but had not thought too much about it. She decided that one thing she could do would be to improve the water system in her schoolroom. She remembered the bucket and dipper that all of the children had used at Orion. At Chester at least all of the children had their own cups, and the school had a water well instead of a cistern. She was sure she could come up with some way to improve her school in that area. Mr. Spenner had each teacher write out a plan to leave with him at the end of the meeting. Helen thought, "Now I really have to do it or tell him the reason why."

C. A. and Helen enjoyed that weekend in October together; it was the first time they had been in Alva as husband and wife. They stayed in C. A.'s room and enjoyed spending time with their old friends.

When Helen got back to Chester, she told Mrs. Jellison about the school-improvement project she had submitted to Mr. Spenner. Mrs. Jellison laughed and said the new superintendent sure did seem to take his job seriously. She said he and Miss Weed checked over all of the school-board records much more closely than Mr. Weaver had done. She said he was awfully fussy about getting his reports completed and submitted to State Superintendent Vaughn on time. Mrs. Jellison agreed to bring up the water project at the next board meeting.

Helen continued to work on the new outlines for the notebooks every evening. She always worked at the kitchen table, where the light was best. She sometimes missed the evenings she had spent with Mrs. Cossell and wished that C. A. could have met her. But time passed quickly and the weekends arrived before she knew it.

In November, Mrs. Jellison told Helen the school board members liked her idea about improving the water system for the children. They said they had no extra money but would help her if they could. Helen talked to her dad and C. A. about the water project. C. A. read the regulations and he and John discussed some possible ways to approach the project and what Helen would need to carry them out. The regulations stated that the school must have a "bubbler fountain or cooler with a faucet outlet with paper cups." The regulation also stated that there must be a trap to prevent the overflow water from returning to the cistern or well. Since they couldn't pipe in water for a bubbler fountain, they decided to develop a cooler. They figured that if she had a wooden keg with a spigot, it would meet the regulations for a sanitary water source. The keg would have to be filled with fresh water every day and all of the children would have to mark their cups so that they wouldn't get them mixed up.

Helen and the children wrote out what they would need on the blackboard. They listed two buckets, one for clean water and one for waste; a small wooden keg that was very clean and didn't leak; a faucet or spigot that was very clean and in good working order; some pegs or nails on which to hang each person's cup; and a dishpan to wash the cups each afternoon before they left school. Helen asked the children to check with their parents to see what they could send to school to help with the project.

Slowly the children brought in what was needed. The first keg smelled of kerosene and couldn't be used. The next keg was too big for them to empty each afternoon. Finally a small keg that had held molasses was brought to school. They were able to scrub it until only a slight sweet taste remained. Helen got one of the men in the community to fit the spigot into it carefully and fix the lid so it could be lifted off, yet fit tightly. As soon as the keg was finished, a couple of the boys took the bucket marked *C* for clean water to the pump and brought in a bucket of fresh water to fill the keg. Then the children got their own cups, which had their initials in red paint, and stood in line to get a cup of water. The bucket marked *W* for waste sat under the spigot to catch the drips. They had to fill the keg three times the first day.

The children of Chester School had their Thanksgiving program and showed their new sanitary water system to the community. Everyone was very proud of what they had accomplished together.

Mr. Spenner came to visit the school early in December. When the children showed him the new water system, he praised them highly. He informed Helen that she had helped Chester become a second-class school. It was not yet a model school but was well on its way, he told her. Helen felt very good about their accomplishments. It might not look like much to other people, but she knew how difficult it was to make any changes. Mr. Spenner did seem to understand and appreciate their efforts. Helen enjoyed working at Chester. She did not miss the isolation or primitiveness of Orion, but she was always glad to see her old friends from that community. A few had managed to come to her school programs that year.

The children planned a very elaborate Christmas program for their school. Helen was excited that C. A. arranged to come down and help her and the children get and decorate their Christmas tree. Helen's whole family came to the program, including her new husband. The community members seemed very happy about their new teacher and the way things were going at Chester School.

Helen and C. A. enjoyed spending the Thanksgiving and Christmas vacations together. They talked about going to Kansas to see his family, but their car was in such bad shape that they didn't want to take a chance of getting too far from home. Helen enjoyed introducing C. A. to all the members of her large extended family. They went to Lahoma to see Helen's mother's parents. C. A. got a big kick out of the Sterbas and enjoyed being in their home. He enjoyed their Bohemian ways with European accents and special foods. The grandparents still spoke Bohemian to each other. They all took to C. A. immediately and were very happy for the young couple.

The time for preparing her children for the county examinations was soon upon Helen. She had six children to be tested that year. Mr. Spenner arranged for her and the teacher from the next school to monitor the testing of the other's pupils. This was the first time Helen had not been involved with the examinations at Fairview. She had to be sure that she gave the correct examinations to the correct child and that she properly signed and mailed the examinations to the superintendent's office. It was a very important job, because the children's schooling and the other teacher's job depended on the outcome.

There were no problems during the examinations.

Helen felt that her pupils had done well, but she missed seeing the other teachers in Fairview. She had been asked to stay at Chester the next year. They were not sure whether C. A. would graduate, so they decided that Helen should stay at Chester another year. Helen liked her school but she grew very tired of the three-mile trip back and forth to Mrs. Jellison's. It was nice to have another twenty dollars per month for themselves, but Helen decided to look for another place to stay the following year.

In the meantime, C. A. found that he was not going to graduate on schedule. He still had to make up a course from the semester that he had taken off for Rochester without withdrawing from school. Helen was disappointed but decided to attend spring term so she could be with C. A. They got a small apartment in which they shared a kitchen and bathroom with another couple. C. A. continued his job at the ice plant and Helen went to school for that term. They worked and played with the other couple, Howard and Bernice, and became very good friends. C. A. completed his requirements and wore his cap and gown to the graduation ceremony in May 1933 at the end of spring term. Helen was very proud of her new husband; no one in her family had graduated from college before. They stayed in Alva for the rest of the summer so that C. A. could continue working. Helen's younger sister Donna, who was to begin college that fall, came up to spend some time with them during the summer. She planned to be a teacher, just like Helen.

When it was time for Helen to return to her school in Chester, C. A. went with her. There were no jobs around Chester, so C. A. went to work for John Hussman on the farm. Helen paid twenty dollars per month for a one-room efficiency in a house right across the road from the school. She had the room all to herself, and C. A. frequently stayed over with her. He was not interested in teaching but did enjoy helping Helen with her programs and fund-raisers. During football season, C. A. would referee for high school games. He had maintained close contact with his football buddies from Alva. What he really wanted to do was to go into the insurance business. He had worked some for an insurance agent in Alva, but business was not good enough to support another man and wife. Helen wasn't too pleased about his aspirations. She couldn't understand why he didn't want to be a teacher.

Throughout the 1933–34 school year, Helen and C. A. discussed what they would do next. The one thing they agreed upon was that Helen would go to school full time to get her degree. She had earned enough credits to be a junior in college and soon would qualify for a five-year certificate: however, with a college degree she would have a lifetime certificate. Helen told the Chester school board that she would not be staying for the following year.

C. A. was enjoying this time working with Helen's father. Not only was John a hard worker, he also was very entertaining. C. A. was learning a lot from him and enjoying their time together. In addition to farming, John raised mules; he had a bunch of brood mares and a jack. The mules didn't go to market until they were three years old, so John often had as many as forty to fifty mules at any one time. He sold them to buyers who passed through on their way to the mule market in Fort Worth, Texas. The mules were used in cotton farming in that part of the country.

John had managed to buy 160 acres along the South Canadian River and had most of it in grass. He kept many of his young mules on the isolated river property, which was six or seven miles south of the farm. Although he went down to check the fences and windmill on horseback, the mules rarely saw a man on foot. If John got off his horse to work on fence or the windmill, they ran as fast as they could to get away from him.

Because mule buyers would pay more for an animal that was broken, John tried to break the three-year-olds before the buyers came in late summer. C. A. began to help John break mules. They drove some mules up from the river to the farm, where they went about breaking them to harness. They then used the mules in the harvest field with the teams of horses. Each mule weighed between nine hundred and eleven hundred pounds by the time it was three years old.

John had fixed up a space in the barn with a narrow stall that was boarded up to the ceiling on three sides. He found that mules could jump and climb over an eight-foot wall. To begin the process, John coaxed the mule into the stall with feed. Then someone would stick two iron bars across the opening just above the back of the mule's knees. John knew that a mule would not bend down and back up, that he would just back up until he felt something. He would give a couple of big kicks and then go forward trying to get out where he could see. After mule wore himself out trying to escape, John would get into the stall with him.

John had a chain harness hooked onto a pulley on the ceiling of the barn. He would pull down the clanging harness and put it over the wild mule's head. He had figured out a way to fasten the harness quickly and would then leave the frightened mule in the stall for a while to get used to the harness. It usually took thirty minutes to an hour to get to this point. John had buried an old disk about four feet under the middle of the barnyard; this was called a deadman. He had left a piece of a chain, which was attached to the disk, sticking out of the ground. To this he had attached an iron ring. When the mule seemed calm enough,

John would tie one end of a strong one-hundred-foot rope to the mule's harness and the other end to the ring. Once the rope was securely fastened, he would remove the iron bars from behind the mule. As soon as the mule realized that he could get out, he would tear out of the barn, running as hard as he could. When he reached the end of the rope, his momentum would cause his feet to fly up into the air and he would land on his back with a terrific thud. The mule would jump up as fast as he could and run just as hard the other way, meeting the same results when he reached the end of his rope. It would usually take three or four times before the mule would be calm enough for John to approach him. At this time, John would get an old mare and keep her between him and the mule as he would slowly walk up the rope toward the mule. If the mule started to run, John would let go of the rope and let him hit the end of it again. If the mule tried to bite or kick, the old mare would take care of him. This had been a very effective way of breaking mules.

In most cases, the mules were not injured during this process; however, one time when C. A. was helping John, the rope got wound around the mule's head. As the mule hit the end of the rope, it pulled against his upper lip and flipped him over. John, C. A., and the others watched as the mule got up and stood there on spraddled, quivering legs with blood running out of his mouth. John walked over to the mule and said, "Well, here's one mule that will get oats the rest of his life." His teeth had been mowed out by the rope. John took out his pocket knife, cut off the teeth that were left dangling, and threw them on the ground. Livestock was valuable and John tried to take very good care of his animals.

The mules were broken to work by being used on teams with horses during harvest. John usually used four head of horses to pull the machinery. After John got a mule broken to lead, he would hitch it up next to a mare. The old mare would keep the young mule in line by biting him or by leaning into him. The old brood mares would actually help break the mules. C. A. was fascinated by what he experienced on the farm; it certainly was different from anything he had done before.

The last two months Helen taught at Chester brought some additional problems for her and C. A. The bank would not cash her warrant from the Chester school board for the full amount, demanding 20 percent of the total if she wanted the money at that time. If she had waited until the school district could collect more taxes, she could possibly have collected all of her money. This turn of events supported C. A.'s contention that teaching school was not as much of a sure-fire thing as Helen had tried to convince him it was.

Helen planned to go to college full time during the 1934–35 school year, so she did not go to summer school. She and C. A. lived on the farm with her parents, and C. A. made periodic trips to Alva to try to get a job in the world of free enterprise. As the summer passed, it became more evident that jobs were very hard to come by. The insurance business was, like everything else at that time, in a big slump.

During the summer, some of the local cowboys came out to the Hussman farm and asked John if they could ride some of his mules. John told them to go ahead, but they couldn't get on even one of the mules. Even with several of them trying to harness a single mule, they were not successful.

John, Helen's brother Ernie, and C. A. watched the scene and laughed loudly. They were always looking for something to give them some fun, so they began to talk about having a mule rodeo. They went out into one of the pastures east of the house and built an arena. They fixed up a gate and a bunch of pens with high sides to keep the mules in. They advertised that the rodeo would be held on a Sunday afternoon. C. A. was the gatekeeper and charged a dollar a carload. They didn't care how many bodies were in or on the car as it went through the gate, it still cost one dollar. Although the times were very hard and the day was very hot, C. A. collected a hundred one-dollar bills that afternoon. They had advertised that they would pay five dollars to anyone who could stay on a mule for ten seconds. The cowboys poured in to collect the big money. That was more than a man could earn in a day—if he was lucky enough to have a job. John had bought several jugs of moonshine, which he had available for free to the riders.

The rodeo began and the cowboys, with visions of five dollars in their heads and several swigs of moonshine in their stomachs, were very aggressive about getting on the mules that were penned in the narrow chutes. However, as soon as the mules were able to move, they jumped, twisted, kicked, and shook off every cowboy in a split second. The cowboys hit the fences and the ground hard. It wasn't long until nobody was willing to get near a mule.

John decided to offer them three dollars to mount a mule and five dollars if they rode it. Only a few entrants decided to take such a chance again, even for three dollars cash money. No one won the five dollars that afternoon. However, they had some other events in the rodeo and they continued with some calf roping, wild-cow milking, and a few other activities with modest prize money. It turned out to be a pretty good rodeo. They cleared almost one hundred dollars in one afternoon. That was a lot of money at that time.

Ernie suggested that they put on another rodeo at the county fair at Taloga. Arrangements were quickly made.

Ernie, John, and C. A. put a couple of old mares in front to lead and on horseback drove the mules the ten miles to Taloga. Ernie and John planned the events for the rodeo, and C. A., who had very little experience in that area, decided that he and Helen would make some extra money for themselves by selling cold drinks. C. A. had worked in carnivals and at athletic events where fruit drinks were sold. They bought two gallons of orange concentrate, some citric acid, some sugar, and some orange coloring. C. A. mixed the ingredients with water in a fifty-gallon drum. The actual cost was very little; C. A. figured that whatever they made would be 95 percent profit. There was a problem deciding what to use for drink containers; however, Stella said she had a lot of extra fruit jars they could have. Helen washed the jars and packed them to take to Taloga. C. A. got a big block of ice from the ice plant and cut it into pieces that were barely small enough to fit in the jars. He knew from working in the carnivals that the larger the chunk of ice, the less drink mix was needed, and the higher the profit would be. They sold the orange drink for ten cents a jar.

That hot, dusty afternoon, Helen and C. A. made over twenty dollars with their drink stand, a lot of money in 1935. Many of the cowboys had been practicing to ride the mules. There were a lot of challenges, but very few could stay on the mules long enough for the prize money. The Hussmans made about eighty dollars that afternoon at their mule rodeo. After the crowd left, Helen and C. A. picked up the empty fruit jars so they could be washed and reused.

They had done so well with the rodeo and the drinks that they decided to put on still another one at Vici, about twenty miles west of the farm. C. A.'s fourteen-year old brother Ernest had arranged to come from Kansas to visit them for a week. He was very excited about taking part in a real rodeo. He loved to ride horses and insisted that he be one of the drivers to take the mules the twenty miles. C. A. was driving over in a car to take the ingredients for his drink stand and tried to persuade Ernest to go over with him. Nothing doing. Ernest insisted that he go with Ernie, Helen's brother, and the other mule drivers. That afternoon there was a terrible windstorm with torrential rains. More than once Ernest wished that he had not started on this venture. However, they eventually got to Vici with the mules.

C. A. and Helen set up their drink stand before the rodeo started. They decided that Ernest could take some jars on a tray and go through the crowd to sell them. They soon discovered that Ernest was not much of a hawker. The ice had melted by the time he returned to tell C. A. that no one wanted to buy any. C. A. gave him fresh drinks and sent him out again after teasing Ernest that he was supposed to sell them, not wait for someone to take them away from him. Finally Ernest returned with several jars gone. He told his brother that he would do anything to help but he just couldn't sell drinks. They decided to let people continue to come to the stand to buy the orange drink. Again C. A. and Helen made about twenty dollars.

This rodeo didn't make as much for the Hussmans as the others had. The audiences had consisted of basically the same people and they were getting tired of seeing the same events. This time the profit was about thirty-five dollars, so they decided to end their rodeo business at Vici. Ernest Morris had a lot of stories to tell his friends in Kansas when he returned from western Oklahoma.

In late summer, the mule buyer came to purchase John's mules. John fed his stock well, so the mules looked very good. The buyer took about sixty-five head at one-hundred dollars per head and hauled them to the sale in Fort Worth. Months later he came back through Seiling and told John he had really taken a beating on those mules. He said that as soon as the mules were driven off the truck and into the pens, they took off like a pack of grayhounds. When the drivers approached them to send them into the sale arena, those crazy mules had jumped over the five-foot fences and had run as hard as they could.

John laughed as he told the folks at home about the mules running away. They decided that the mules had been afraid that they were going to be in another rodeo and wanted no part of it. Most of the people at the mule auction wanted an old plow mule that would just walk along and swing his ears. They sure didn't want a mule that would jump a five-foot fence and run like a deer. John hoped the mule buyer would be back the next year.

By the end of the summer, Helen's sister Donna had taken a job teaching at a school near Chester. C. A. found it impossible to get a job of any kind in Alva. The state of Oklahoma had a surplus of teachers, Helen heard.[1] In desperation, she contacted Mr. Spenner at Fairview. He told her there were only a few openings but Orion School was still looking for a teacher.

Helen was determined not to repeat the pattern of the previous two years of their marriage. There weren't any other jobs around for C. A., and they could not continue to live on the farm with her parents. At her insistence, C. A. accepted the job at Orion School for a salary of eighty dollars per month, but only with the understanding that he would not have to stay there alone while Helen attended school at Alva. They had bought a used 1934 Ford sedan at Fairview, but they knew it would eat up their money to drive back and forth to Seiling or Chester if they lived there.

RETURN TO ORION SCHOOL

Living in a Tent

Helen and C. A. went to John for suggestions about their dilemma in finding an acceptable place to live.[1] John told them that many of the first settlements, especially after the land runs as Oklahoma was being settled, had been made up of tents. He informed them that he and Stella still had a tent they had used for camping. Helen remembered the trip to Colorado and the green tent they had stayed in. John said the tent could be put on a wooden floor and fitted with wooden walls to make a fairly substantial structure. It could also be waterproofed, he said. After several discussions and a trip to Orion, they decided to put the tent across the road from the school so that they could use the school's cistern and outhouses.

Early in September, John and C. A. went to Orion to put up the nine-by-twelve-foot tent. They chose a flat place among the blackjacks so that the trees would form a wind-break. They put down a wooden floor and boarded up the walls for about three feet. Then they stretched the tent over the top and brushed on a mixture of paraffin and gasoline. This was to make sure the tent would never sweat or leak in a hard rain.

Helen had visualized having to bend down and crawl

141

under a tent flap to get into her new home. She was pleasantly surprised to see that her husband and her dad had made a real door with a little glass window in it for her. There were no other windows, so they had wanted her to be able to see out.

Although Donna had been getting ready for her first year of teaching, she took time to help Helen and Stella get things ready for Helen's and C. A.'s new home. Helen decided their color was going to be green. She and her sister papered the board walls with a green print wallpaper and used the same paper on the wooden frame supporting the tent. Helen sewed little cloth pockets which she fastened to the wooden wall all around the sides of the tent. In the pockets she and C. A. kept their clothes, shoes, and underwear. They made a small clothes closet by putting up a curtain.

Their nine-by-twelve-foot home was furnished with a sanitary cot, which could have one or both sides up or down; a wooden drop-leaf table with two chairs; two orange crates with a board between them to form a workspace on top and storage underneath; a small cookstove that had been a salesman's sample; and assorted cooking utensils, buckets, pans, and a coal-oil lamp. Helen was eager to play the role of housewife. After all, she and C. A. had been married for two years and this was their first home. They would live in this tent until May 1935.

C. A. had a bachelor of science degree and a lifetime certificate and was making only eighty dollars a month in 1934–35. In contrast, Helen, with a third-grade certificate, had made eighty-five dollars at the same school in 1931–32. But they were glad that C. A. had a job. During the football season, he continued to referee the Friday games. Helen would substitute-teach for him so that he could make five to six dollars per game and be able to continue with some of the things he enjoyed. The courses he had taken at college had not prepared him for teaching in a one-room school. His degree was in history and physical education. He had not even attended a one-room school as a child. However, he was a willing learner and Helen had five years of teaching experience. She gave him all of her teaching materials, although she was also working with her sister Donna, who was teaching at Chester. Helen made the new outlines for the textbooks that had been adopted that year, but tried to stay out of the schoolroom as much as possible. In the two years since she had left Orion there were some new children, but many of them she knew.

The children loved C. A. from the first day. They liked his outgoing personality and enjoyed his storytelling. He had eighteen pupils in grades 1 through 8 and two beginners. When it was time for C. A. to listen to the beginners read, he would lift each of them onto one of his knees. Recitation time became very special for them. All of the children enjoyed the way their teacher played with them at recess and lunchtime. Often one of the children would go and get Helen so that there could be an adult on each side. As it began to get colder, Helen suggested that she again fix soup for lunch. In the mornings after C. A. had the stove started, she would go over to the school and put whatever was available into the soup pot. At lunchtime she would return to eat with the children and C. A. and to help them clean up.

Helen and C. A. found that although they could keep each other warm, everything else in the tent froze at night once the weather turned cold. They decided to dig a three-by-three-foot cave near the tent. They lined it with evergreen boughs and got a wooden top for it. At night they put limbs

C. A. Morris with twelve of his eighteen pupils at Orion School in 1934.

on top to help keep it from freezing and to keep the coyotes out. In the cave Helen kept her starter for bread, vegetables, canned fruit from Stella, and any meat that they had salted.

Helen joined a home demonstration club that year. She attended the monthly meetings and became more involved with the people in the community. She enjoyed the role of the teacher's wife.

On many evenings, Helen and C. A. went hunting with C. A.'s .22-caliber rifle. Squirrels and rabbits were plentiful and they could quickly get enough meat for themselves and for the children's lunch stew. C. A. usually brought a bucket of water when he came home from school. They took sponge baths with the washpan and threw the wastewater out the door. They continued to use the school's outhouses. These were the best quarters Helen had ever had around Orion, even if she was living in a tent.

Helen always made C. A. sleep on the side of the cot next to the wall, because they could hear the coyotes sniffing around outside of the tent at night. Helen always made sure that any leftovers were tightly sealed in jars, but the coyotes always seemed hopeful that they would find more than a scent in the air. That year, the coyotes did not bother anything except Helen's sleep.

They renewed their friendship with the Holubs, who now had a little girl. Each couple would go to the other's house for dinner or to play cards. In the tent, two would sit on the chairs and two would sit on the cot. The little girl would usually go to sleep on the cot before her parents were ready to leave the Morrises' cozy home. The little Holub girl liked to perform for them. At some point in the evening, they would get out the syrup bucket for her to stand on while she sang little songs that she had been taught.

They continued to go to the Hussman's often. Helen would take the dirty clothes she had not been able to wash in her small washpan and use her mother's washhouse, which was equipped with washtubs, scrubboards, a water pump, and a stove to heat the water. It was also a chance for C. A. and Helen to take a bath in a full-size tub, although they still had to carry and heat water from the cistern.

One weekend Stella's brother and his family were visiting the Hussmans from Oklahoma City. They had heard so much about C. A.'s and Helen's tent that they insisted on coming over to Orion for an evening. The weather was very cold, but by the time all twelve people got into the tent, they were quite warm. People sat on buckets, the floor—any place they could find space. It was a fairly short evening, but they all had a good time.

C. A. began to plan for his first fund-raiser, to be held in early October. He had attended Helen's in the past and had noticed how many people came early, occupied the best seats during the program, and then left without spending any money at all. He decided he would not allow that to happen. C. A. advertised that it would cost ten cents to attend Orion's pie and box supper. For the admission price, there would be professional entertainers and all the coffee you could drink. Several people in the community told C. A. he was making a big mistake and no one would come. He told them that if no one came, he would do it the other way next time.

On the night of the pie and box supper, C. A. had some of his musician friends from Alva come to the school early. They often played for dances around Alva and had volunteered their services for the evening to their old friend. They played modern dance music on guitars and a fiddle. As people pulled up to the school, they could hear the music playing. Everyone was willing to pay the ten-cent admission fee for the extras. As the time came to auction the boxes and pies, they were willing to pay more money than usual for them, too. Although times were very hard, people spent as much as they could for their school and for their own entertainment.

C. A. had worked with older children on some little woodworking projects. They made doorstops, message boards, and animals out of wooden apple crates from the grocery store. They painted them and were selling them for ten and fifteen cents each. Before the evening was over, they had sold them all.

Only one thing happened that night that C. A. and Helen regretted. Times were so hard that people in the community had very little to bring in their boxes. One lady brought a huge popcorn ball. The price on this unique item was very high; however, when the unlucky buyer got partway into the ball, he found that the center was filled with cotton. The confronted patron laughed and reminded him that the money was for the school. The man was not happy, but he did not ask for his money back. That evening, C. A. raised more than twenty-five dollars for Orion School.

Mr. Hedrick, who was again on the school board, told C. A. that it had been the most successful fund-raiser in the entire county. Donna asked if she could borrow the patterns and the coping saw so that her children could make some of the wooden items for their next fund-raiser. The community was very pleased with the job C. A. was doing at Orion School.

He became very concerned about the children who didn't have adequate clothing that winter. One weekend, he and his brother-in-law Ernie went to Vici to a sale, bought a large batch of shoes and clothing, and hauled it to Orion School. On Monday morning, the children had a lot of fun picking out clothes they could wear. Although many of the shoes were high-top button styles, they did find some clothes that would keep them warm as the cruel winter wind whipped across the prairie and along the canyon rim. C. A. cut the high heels off some of the ladies' shoes so that the children could wear them. The little children spent many happy hours during lunches and recesses that winter playing dress-up in the remaining clothes.

That spring Helen's cousin Lil came from Kansas to visit Helen and C. A. She stayed with them for a week in their little tent home. They raised the second side of their sanitary cot, which made a three-quarters bed. Helen slept in the middle with C. A. against the wall and Lil on the inside. Helen and Lil had a good time talking and visiting around the community during the day. During the evenings, Lil would go out with her boyfriend, who lived nearby. Often Helen and C. A. would be in bed when Lil returned from her dates. Lil's visit was a warm memory for all of them for many years to come.

Helen helped prepare the Orion children for the county examinations. She worked with the pupils who had to take examinations as C. A. taught the other children. Helen also helped Donna prepare her pupils for tests. The time flew. Helen decided that she would definitely attend the spring session at Northwestern State Teachers College beginning in May. She could qualify for her five-year certificate if she took the spring and summer terms. Therefore, she would have to leave C. A. at Orion to finish out the last few days of school and to take care of tearing down the tent and moving their belongings back to the Hussman farm. C. A. had given notice to the school board that he would not be staying for another year. Helen and he would spend the summer figuring out what they would do next.

At the end of April, they were surprised to discover that the bank would not cash the warrant from Orion without charging the 20 percent fee. Although the district had always been able to pay its teachers before, the times were getting too hard and taxes were difficult to collect. C. A. was tempted to end school early, as many other teachers did, so that he could go to Alva with Helen. However, he knew it was not the children's fault, so he took Helen to Alva and settled her into a little apartment and returned to Orion by himself. He finished out the school year, but was never paid his last warrant.

After school was out, John came over to help his son-in-law take down the tent. They loaded everything into a truck and took it to the farm. They had borrowed almost everything from the Hussmans, so there were few things that C. A. had to worry about storing or moving to Alva.

C. A. went to Alva, where he worked in the creamery while Helen went to classes at the college. They again shared space with their friends, Howard and Bernice, who were also in school. The summer passed with no job prospects for C. A.

At the end of the August term, to celebrate Helen's qualifying for the five-year certificate, they decided to go to the 1935 World's Fair in Chicago. John Hussman had ridden the train to the livestock sales in Chicago several times and had told them a lot about the big city. Helen had never been to any big city and really wanted to go to the fair. They had saved seventy dollars from C. A.'s summer job and agreed to stay within that budget. The young couple drove to Chicago in their old car and for seven dollars rented a room in a private home near the fairgrounds for a week. They had a key to the door so that they could come and go as they wished. Using the fair brochure, they planned out their visit on a day-to-day basis. They were able to stay within their budget and see all of the sights.

On the way back to Oklahoma from the fair, C. A. told Helen that he had decided to teach again the following year. Helen, knowing that he was very good with children, was happy to hear about his decision. She realized this would mean that she would have to postpone her desire to be a full-time student and finish her degree. She wondered whether they would be able to find jobs close together for the next year. It was getting awfully late in the year to find two teaching positions.

They went to the county superintendent's office as soon

as they could get to Fairview. Mr. Spenner's face lit up when he heard they would both be teaching that year. He asked if they would like to take the two-room school at Cimarron Valley near Ringwood. Helen couldn't believe their good fortune. Not only would they have jobs together, but this was also quite a step up from Orion School. One drawback would be the thirty-mile distance they would be from her parents. Helen knew that she would have to grow up and stop depending on them so much, and this was a good time to begin.

Cimarron Valley was a consolidated school which had been organized on May 10, 1924, from four districts. The other school buildings had been torn down and sold to pay for the construction of the new school, which had been constructed to meet the state building codes. The school had two buses and, best of all, a teacherage. Their salaries would be one hundred forty dollars per month plus the teacherage. The school year was 160 days.

S I X

A HUSBAND-WIFE TEACHING TEAM

The young couple went right over to meet with the school board at one of the members' homes near Cimarron Valley School and were hired. They were delighted with the two spacious classrooms and a folding door which would allow them to have one big room for programs. Under the bell tower was an entry foyer with cloakrooms on each side. Heat was generated by a woodstove in the basement and rose through grates in the floor of each room. The windows in the classrooms were on the north side and extended from three feet above the floor to six inches from the ceiling. The areas below the windows were covered with wainscoting which extended all along the outside walls. Each classroom had an emergency exit door at the end of the room. It was an exciting change for Helen and C. A., who had been teaching in primitive buildings which were erected in the late 1800s. There were outhouses, but these met the state requirements for sanitation and improved design.

The teacherage provided them with their first house. It consisted of a small living room, a small bedroom, and a kitchen. They had no furniture, so they made a trip to Enid to buy furnishings for their new home. Helen's new green enamel kerosene cookstove could bake biscuits in twelve

151

minutes. No more cooking on a woodstove for her! For several days, Helen just walked around, touching the new table and chairs and living-room and bedroom furniture. According to their agreement, the teachers had to furnish their own wood for the wood heating stove provided in the teacherage.

There were ninety pupils in the school, fifty of them in the first three grades. Helen taught the primary children in grades 1 through 3 and C. A. taught the others. Most of the children rode one of the two school buses operated by the district. There was a state effort to improve transportation at that time. Although the facility was much better and there were many more instructional materials, Helen and C. A. were not accustomed to meeting the demands of so many children. Because they had more children and fewer grades to teach, they devised some teaching methods with more group work.

C. A. made a little workshop in the basement, although there was barely room for him to stand up straight. He also coached the boys' and girls' basketball teams. Their practice sessions and home games were played on the sand court behind the school. The teams did not have uniforms, so they played in cut-off pants and regular shirts. There was a 4-H Club sponsored by the county agent. Children were excused from school to attend the meetings, and many participated in the fairs and shows related to the 4-H Club.

Helen organized the monthly literary programs and found that the community was very active. The large double room was always filled to capacity for every program. Unlike those in her other schools, these patrons were interested in more intellectually stimulating programs, not just the performances of their children. There was no other center for community activities, because the nearest church was in Ringwood.

The patrons were very happy to have Mr. and Mrs. Morris as their teachers. In fact, Helen and C. A. had difficulty finding privacy. Someone from the community would stop by almost every evening. Frequently they would bring their supper with them, or sometimes a dessert of ice cream or cake. They were very generous people and would share their garden and farm products with the teachers. C. A. and Helen tried to go to Seiling once a month unless her parents stopped by on their way to or from Lahoma.

Cimarron Valley School had a much larger operating budget than did the other schools in which they had worked. The geographic area for taxes was four times larger, and the district had the additional income from a railroad that crossed the southern part of the district.

C. A. decided that his boys' basketball team was going to be good enough to get into the tournament at Fairview. They practiced and played their home games on the sand court behind the school. None of their opponents had courts that were any better. It was a game of pass and shoot. C. A. told the boys on the team that he wanted them to look as good as they played, and they began a project to buy uniforms for the team. Since there were a lot of blackjack oak trees around and most homes still had woodstoves, they planned to chop wood and sell it. Parents provided the truck after school and on Saturdays. One of the community members gave them permission to use his land, and they began working hard at basketball and chopping wood. They were winning their games and they were selling their wood.

Shortly before the tournament, the new uniforms arrived. It was a very proud team that went to Fairview to the tournament, and a very proud coach watched them bring home the trophy. The girls' team had not played nearly as well and still did not have uniforms; however, they were very proud of the boys' team and vowed to work harder so they would have a better team the next year.

Although the community at Cimarron Valley was very active, there was no increase in the amount of contact with the Major County superintendent. C. A. and Helen attended the teachers' meetings and Mr. Spenner made his annual visit, but, as usual, they were on their own for the day-to-day responsibilities they had.

Helen and C. A. decided to visit his parents for Christmas that year and left for Kansas the day after the school Christmas program. They were still driving their old car, which wasn't too dependable anymore. Although the weather was good on their trip to Kansas, it became very cold on the way home. They did not have a heater in their car, so they were burning

Helen Morris with her pupils in grades 1 through 3 at Cimarron Valley School.

some small candles on the dashboard to defrost the windshield. The back seat was loaded with their suitcases, Christmas presents, and some canned goods that C. A.'s mother had given them. He had especially liked her homemade ketchup, so she had given him several quarts.

About halfway back to Cimarron Valley, the car hit a slick spot and flipped over. The jars of ketchup broke, spilling the thick red sauce all over everything, including Helen's head. C. A. got out quickly and ran around to the passenger side to check on Helen. Some men who had seen the wreck came running up to help. When they pulled Helen out of the car door, she was holding her hands over one of her eyes. The men thought she had been seriously injured and was covered with blood, because the windshield had shattered and glass was everywhere. They soon realized that the red stuff was ketchup, not blood, and began to wipe it off.

C. A. Morris with his pupils in grades 4 through 8 at Cimarron Valley School in 1936.

C. A. got Helen's hand away from her eye and discovered that a piece of tobacco from his cigarette had got into her eye and was burning like the dickens. Using a clean handkerchief, he got the tobacco out of her eye while the men turned their car back over onto its wheels. They poked all of the ketchup-covered mess into the back seat and discovered that the car would still run. With no windshield, but with thankfulness that neither of them had been hurt, they started on for Cimarron Valley and their home. Days later, Helen was finally able to get the red, sticky ketchup off everything in the car. Some of the patrons helped C. A. put in a new windshield, and life returned to normal.

C. A. had ten pupils who were to take the county examinations that spring. He worked very hard to get their notebooks finished so that they could do the drill work on Saturdays. Helen didn't help much up to this point, because

C. A. Morris with his winning boys' basketball team from Cimarron Valley School in 1936.

C. A. Morris with the girls' basketball team from Cimarron Valley School in 1936.

she had her hands full with fifty primary children to teach every day; however, she did help during the Saturday drill sessions. The buses didn't run on Saturdays, so parents or neighbors had to bring the children to the school. Sometimes after the sessions, Helen and C. A. would take a stranded pupil or two home in their old car.

Six of C. A.'s pupils passed the examinations that year. On May 1, 1936, a rural-school commencement program for Major County was held in Fairview for the 147 graduates from the eighth grade. The 6 pupils from Cimarron Valley and one from Orion made Helen and C. A. feel very good about their teaching experience. However, C. A. still wanted to try to make a career in the insurance business. He had maintained a relationship with the friend in Alva and had been offered a chance to sell burial insurance. They would leave Cimarron Valley School.

EPILOGUE

Helen's parents planned to go to California during the summer of 1936. Helen's sisters, Donna, who was now married to Art, and Laurena, who was also married, were going with their parents. They begged Helen to go along, too. Helen decided to do so and let C. A. see whether he could make a go of the insurance business. She felt quite sure that, with her five-year certificate and six years of teaching experience, she could get a teaching job in almost any community that C. A. would wind up in.

While they were on the trip to California, Helen discovered that she was pregnant. There would be no teaching for her the next year. An elated C. A. suggested that they live in Alva so that he could give the insurance job a real try and also pick up some part-time jobs to help make ends meet. Helen gave birth to a son, John, on February 2, 1937, and never returned to formal teaching or to college to complete her degree. C. A. returned to teaching in a large consolidated high school in Piedmont, Oklahoma, where another son, Tom, and a daughter, Donna, were born. In 1942, C. A. left teaching for good and became an Oklahoma Highway Patrol trooper. He took military leave from the patrol to serve in the U.S. Navy during World War II and returned after the war to work with the Highway Patrol until retirement in 1964. Although they had lived in several other Oklahoma towns, C. A. and Helen remained in Enid after moving there in 1955.

In 1984, Helen and C. A. attended a reunion of the Orion School pupils. They thoroughly enjoyed sharing their memories of the years they spent in that area, especially the year in the tent. In March of 1985, a few months before he and Helen would celebrate their fifty-third wedding anniversary, C. A. died of heart failure.

Although Helen spent most of their married years as a housewife and mother, she did work for several years in a child day-care facility and for part of one year in a school cafeteria. After C. A.'s death, she decided she should spend at least part of her time helping others. In 1987, at seventy-seven years of age, Helen was working one day a week in a nursing home, delivering mail, helping patients write letters, and just visiting with them. She also began training to be a volunteer reading tutor in an elementary school near her home.

Orion School, District 203, was dissolved on July 16, 1947, after ten redistricting changes. Chester School, District 38, was closed on July 16, 1947, when it was consolidated with Dewey County School District C–8. The location of the two school buildings could not be verified in 1986. Cimarron Valley School, Consolidated District 6, which had been established on May 10, 1924, was divided between two other consolidated districts on June 25, 1968, and the building was converted into a family home.

Helen Hussman Morris and C. A. Morris in formal photographs taken while they were teaching at Cimarron Valley School in 1935–36.

NOTES

INTRODUCTION: A BRIEF HISTORY OF
PUBLIC EDUCATION IN OKLAHOMA

1. Council of Chief State School Officers, p. 981.

2. *Fourteenth Biennial Report of Oklahoma Department of Education* (1932–1936), p. 1.

3. Council of Chief State School Officers, p. 978.

4. *Fourteenth Biennial Report of Oklahoma Department of Education* (1932–36), p. 1.

5. Ibid.

6. Council of Chief State School Officers, p. 979.

7. Warren, p. 44.

8. Council of Chief State School Officers, pp. 984–85.

9. *Thirteenth Biennial Report of the Superintendent of Public Instruction of the State of Oklahoma,* p. 126, and Gulliford, p. 70.

10. Gulliford, p. 41.

11. Council of Chief State School Officers, pp. 979, 985.

12. Ibid., p. 980.

13. Ibid., p. 985.

14. Ibid.

15. Ibid.

16. Ibid., p. 984.

17. Ibid., p. 989.

18. *Sixteenth Biennial Report of Oklahoma Department of Education* (1932–36), p. 115.

19. Council of Chief State School Officers, p. 981.

20. *Thirteenth Biennial Report,* p. 21.

21. Council of Chief State School Officers, p. 981.

22. *Thirteenth Biennial Report,* p. 148.

23. *Sixteenth Biennial Report of Oklahoma Department of Education* (1932–36), p. 88.

24. Ibid.

25. Ibid., pp. 86–87.

26. *Fifteenth Biennial Report of Oklahoma Department of Education* (1932–36), p. 21.

27. Ibid., p. 153.

28. *Fourteenth Biennial Report of Oklahoma Department of Education* (1932–36), p. 98.

29. *Bulletins 1931,* p. 6.

30. *Fourteenth Biennial Report of Oklahoma Department of Education* (1932–36), p. 99.

31. Council of Chief State School Officers, p. 982.

32. Gulliford, pp. 68–69.

33. Ibid., pp. 68–69.

Prologue

1. *Thirteenth Biennial Report,* pp. 127–28, gives a detailed description of the county examinations.

CHAPTER 1. HELEN BECOMES A TEACHER

1. Gulliford, pp. 70–71, and *Thirteenth Biennial Report,* pp. 124–26, give information related to teacher certification by examination.

2. Oklahoma School Act of 1931. Article IV cites the 1929 law that required the county superintendent to collect the two-dollar fee from each applicant and deliver it to the county treasurer.

3. Ibid. Section 54 of Article III required all teachers in the state to subscribed to the following oath: "I (name) do solemnly swear (or affirm) that I will support, obey, and defend the Constitution of the United States, and the constitution of the State of Oklahoma." Section 53 states that the written contract between each school district and each qualified teacher had to specify the wages per week or per month. The teacher could be dismissed for incompetence, cruelty, negligence, or immorality. It was unlawful for any school district to employ a person to teach who was related to a member of the school board.

4. The Record of Change in School District Boundaries, kept in the superintendent's office in the Major County Courthouse,

describes the establishment of each school district in the county and all changes in boundaries that occurred. Betts, Gulliford, and *Fourteenth Biennial Report,* p. 1, describe the one-room schools that were built in the 1890s.

5. Oklahoma law provided that children whose parents were unable to purchase the required textbooks would have them furnished at the expense of the county in which they resided.

6. Oklahoma School Act of 1931, Article V, section 91.

7. Ibid., Article XXXVII, lists these general provisions in great detail.

8. The school laws of Oklahoma in 1928–1930 contained provisions for the compulsory attendance of all pupils between the ages of eight and eighteen for at least two-thirds of the school term in the districts in which they resided. The following groups of students were exempt: (1) those who had satisfactorily completed the courses of instruction in the districts in which they resided, and (2) those who had satisfactorily completed the eighth grade and were regularly and lawfully employed.

9. *Thirteenth Biennial Report* suggested the following reasons for poorer attendance in rural schools: muddy roads, distance from school, uncomfortable buildings, necessity to help with farm work, and moving from one farm to another during the school term.

10. Oklahoma school law passed in 1925.

11. Oklahoma School Act of 1931, Article III, section 60 and Article XXVIII, section 359 describe the roles of county superintendents and district school boards in obtaining state-approved registers, record books, and forms and making sure that every teacher and school board used them according to state regulations.

12. Ibid., Article XXXVII, describes these special days and the regulations for the observance of each.

13. Under state school law, it was the duty of the county superintendent to visit each school in his county at least once each school term of six months and correct any deficiencies in the running of the school, the classification of pupils, or the method of instruction; to make suggestions in private to the teachers "as he shall deem proper and necessary to the welfare of the school"; to note the character and condition of the schoolhouse, furniture, apparatus, and grounds; and to make a written report to the district school board. It should be noted that there was no provision for the teacher to see the report.

14. The Oklahoma School Act of 1931 stated that the district must provide the necessary supplies during the time school was in session.

15. Gulliford, pp. 192–93, describes the interior of the one-room schools in great detail.

16. Betts and Hall, p. 165, state that "the rural teacher has only himself to depend on. For the help that can be rendered by the board is negligible, and the county superintendent is too far away and his visits are too rare to be immediate assistance when needed. . . . But the daily problems of the district school must all be met by the rural teacher as they arise, and on the basis of his own judgement. To be successful, the rural teacher must therefore have a ready knowledge of the principles underlying the three great fields of problems connected with his work—he must understand clearly the organization, the management and the teaching of the rural school."

17. Gulliford, pp. 48–49, describes thoroughly the procedure and routines used in one-room schools.

18. Gulliford, p. 49, states that a teacher had to prepare lessons to accommodate the learning ability and progress of each child. With a school full of pupils who ranged from six to sixteen years old, a teacher giving instruction in all of the subjects required by the state had to prepare a variety of individual lessons. The teacher could prepare similar assignments and drills for the nine-year-olds, but students who were fourteen required different lessons, as did those who were six or twelve. A teacher with twenty students of varying ages and skills had to prepare as many as forty daily lessons.

19. Gulliford, p. 50, describes the morning recess.

20. Gulliford, p. 50, describes the transition from one subject to another in one-room schools.

21. Gulliford, pp. 74–77, states that some of the nonteaching responsibilities of teachers were sweeping, scrubbing, mopping, dusting, and blackboard washing. They also had to take responsibility for bringing in wood and buckets of water. Country teachers had to be prepared to cope with emergencies, such as snakes and storms. He concludes that, "inexperienced or not, the teacher was expected to be knowledgeable in all areas, ever-responsible, sincere, and courageous."

22. Gulliford, pp. 50–51, describes lunchtime and school-yards.

23. Oklahoma School Act of 1931, Article II, section 59 notes that "the teacher may suspend from the privileges of a school any pupil guilty of immorality or persistent violations of the regulations of the school. Provided, that the pupil suspended shall have the right to appeal from the decision of the said teacher to the board of directors, which shall, upon a full investigation of the charges preferred against said pupil, determine as to the guilt or innocence of the offense charged, and their decision shall be final."

24. Gulliford, p. 48.

25. Oklahoma School Act of 1931, Article II, section 105 decreed that the qualified voters in each district would determine the length of time school would be taught in their districts. However, it was not to be less than three months.

26. The state law identifying Temperance Day as a special day for schools was passed in 1929.

27. *Fifteenth Biennial Report of Oklahoma Department of Education* (1932–36), p. 21, notes that in the 1930–31 school year six Oklahoma counties had supervisors of rural schools but in 1931–32 only three of these counties employed special supervisors.

28. Until the trip to the Major County Courthouse in the summer of 1986, Helen had never seen the records that county superintendents had made of their observations of her during their annual visits to her schools.

29. William H. ("Alfalfa Bill") Murray was the controversial governor of Oklahoma from 1931 to 1935.

30. Oklahoma School Act of 1931. Sections 525 and 526 of Article XXXVII identify the day on which Arbor Day was to be observed and the manner in which it was to be observed in every school.

31. Gulliford, pp. 47–48.

32. Oklahoma School Act of 1931, Article II, section 17, required the county superintendent to keep his office in the county seat open on Saturday of each week; in counties in which he or she had a clerk or assistant, the office was to be kept open all days of the week.

33. Ibid., Article I, section 6, describes in detail the report the state superintendent was to submit to the governor on the first day of December preceding each regular session of the legislature.

34. Ibid., Article III, section 44, gives a detailed description of the reports each school board was to submit to the legal voters for

approval and then to the county superintendent by the first day of August of each year.

35. Ibid., Article III, section 37 lists the qualifications of school board members.

36. *Thirteenth Biennial Report, p. 197.*

CHAPTER 2. HARD TIMES COME TO ORION

1. The photographs of Helen and the children show the merry-go-round.

2. American Association of School Administrators, p. 174, notes that "one of the fine possibilities for enriching the curriculum in the small school is the exchange of assembly programs among several schools. . . . The purpose of the exchange program should be to create friendship and cooperation between schools and to train pupils as listeners."

3. Oklahoma School Act of 1931. Article III, section 38 states the oath of office for district officers: "I, _____ , hereby declare, under oath, that I will faithfully perform the duties of _____ school district _____ , county of _____ ,to the best of my ability and that I will faithfully discharge all the duties pertaining to said office and obey the constitution and laws of the United States and of Oklahoma."

CHAPTER 3. ROMANCE LEADS TO MARRIAGE

1. *Fifteenth Biennial Report of Oklahoma Department of Education* (1932–36), pp. 172–73, lists the distribution of state aid by county from 1927–28 to 1933–34, including transfer fees paid by the state. Distribution of federal aid also is included.

CHAPTER 4. HELEN MOVES TO CHESTER SCHOOL

1. *Fifteenth Biennial Report of Oklahoma Department of Education* (1932–36), pp. 153–56, noted that although there had been a budget reduction of 30 percent at the six teachers' colleges, there was a surplus of teachers in the state.

CHAPTER 5. RETURN TO ORION SCHOOL: LIVING IN A TENT

1. Gulliford, pp. 68–69, describes the difficulties encountered in rural communities as teachers attempted to find housing.

Bibliography

GENERAL PUBLICATIONS

Agar, M. H. *The Professional Stranger: An Informal Introduction to Ethnog-raphy.* New York: Academic Press, 1980.

American Association of School Administrators. *Schools in Small Commu-nities.* Seventeenth Yearbook. Washington, D.C.: American Associa-tion of School Administrators, 1939.

Barker, B., Muse, I., and Smith, R. "One-Teacher Schools in America Today." Paper presented at seventy-sixth annual conference of the Rural Education Association at Olympia, Washington, in October 1984.

Betts, G. H., and Hall, O. E. *Better Rural Schools.* Indianapolis: Bobbs-Merrill Co., 1914.

Bogden, R. C., and Biklen, S. K. *Qualitative Research for Education: An Introduction to Theory and Methods.* Boston: Allyn and Bacon, 1982.

Bryan Kohnstamm, B. "Second Aspen Institute Features Foxfire's Wiggin-ton." *Country Teacher,* October 1987.

Campbell, R. F., Bridges, E. M., and Nystrand, R. O. *Introduction to Educa-tional Administration.* Fifth edition. Boston: Allyn and Bacon, 1977.

Council of Chief State School Officers. *Education in the States: Historical Development and Outlook.* Ed. by J. B. Pearson and E. Fuller. Washing-ton, D.C.: National Education Association of the United States, 1969.

Deering, G. H., ed. *Look at Oklahoma.* Bicentennial edition. Oklahoma City: Oklahoma Publishing Co., 1975.

Gaumnitz, W. H. "Status of Teachers and Principals Employed in the Rural Schools of the United States." U.S. Department of the Interior, Office of Education, *Bulletin 1932, No. 3.* Washington, D.C.: Government Printing Office, 1932.

Gulliford, A. *America's Country Schools.* Washington, D.C.: Preservation Press, 1984.

Hughes, W. A., Sr. "The One-Teacher School: A Disappearing Institution." U.S. Department of Educational Research and Improvement Historical Report, January 1986.

Kindley, M. M. "Little Schools on the Prairie Still Teach a Big Lesson." *Smithsonian Magazine,* October 1985.

Miles, M. B., and Huberman, A. M. *Qualitative Data Analysis: A Sourcebook of New Methods.* Beverly Hills, Calif.: Sage Publications, 1984.

Morris, J. W., and McReynolds, E. C. *Historical Atlas of Oklahoma.* Norman: University of Oklahoma Press, 1965.

National Education Association. *One-Teacher Schools Today.* Research Monograph 1960-MI. Washington, D.C.: NEA Research Division, 1960.

National Society for the Study of Education. *Education in Rural Communities: Fifty-first yearbook, Part II.* Ed. by Nelson B. Henry. Chicago: University of Chicago Press, 1952.

Rand McNally and Co. Oklahoma Road Map. Printed for Champlain Oil Co., 1964.

Shirk, G. H. *Oklahoma Place Names.* Norman: University of Oklahoma Press, 1974.

U.S. Department of Education. *Statistics of State School Systems; Statistics of Public Elementary and Secondary School Systems; Statistics of Nonpublic Elementary and Secondary Schools.* Washington, D.C.: National Center for Education Statistics, 1982.

Warren, D. R. *To Enforce Education.* Detroit: Wayne State University Press, 1974.

VOLUMES FROM THE OKLAHOMA DEPARTMENT OF EDUCATION

Biennial Reports of Oklahoma Department of Education, Vol. 3, 1924–1932. Assistant State Superintendent.

Biennial Reports of Oklahoma Department of Education. Vol. 3, 1932–1936. High School Inspection.

Biennial Reports of Oklahoma Department of Education, Vol. 4, 1934–1938. Assistant State Superintendent.

Thirteenth Biennial Report of the Superintendent of Public Instruction of the State of Oklahoma. July 1, 1928, to June 30, 1930.

Oklahoma Department of Education Bulletins, 1931. State Superintendent.

LEDGERS IN THE MAJOR COUNTY COURT HOUSE

Accredited Schools (miscellaneous information in poor condition).
County Superintendent Yearbook, 1928–1936.
Examination Record Eighth Grade, 1929–1957.
Record of Apportionment School Fund.
Record of Change in School District Boundaries.
Record of Retirement Warrants, 1940–1970.
Record of School District Officers, 1907–1939.
Record of Superintendents Visits, 1907–1934.
Record of Teacher's Certificates.
Register of Teachers Employed.
Teachers' Employment Record, 1941–1960.
Yearbook, 1937–1942.

OTHER RECORDS IN THE MAJOR COUNTY COURTHOUSE

Enumeration Records.
Permanent Grade Records, Including Graduates of Accredited Schools and
    Elementary School Records.

INDEX